Assessing
Student Centred
Courses

Graham Gibbs

© Oxford Centre for Staff Development 1995

Published by
THE OXFORD CENTRE FOR STAFF DEVELOPMENT
Oxford Brookes University
Gipsy Lane
Headington
Oxford
OX3 0BP

Assessing Student Centred Courses
ISBN 1 873576 39 0
British Library Cataloguing-in-Publication Data.
A catalogue record for this book is available from the British Library.

Designed and Typeset in Palatino and Helvetica Narrow by Dan Barker

Printed in Great Britain by
Oxonian Rewley Press Ltd
Oxford

Printed on paper produced from sustainable forests.

Contents

Foreword

This publication is the outcome of one of the last acts of the Council for National Academic Awards, the CNAA, when it funded a project entitled 'Assessment methods for student centred courses' in 1992. It is common for innovation in assessment to lag behind innovation in teaching and learning methods and the development of appropriate assessment methods has often followed a long way behind the introduction of student centred courses. This problem was identified by the CNAA in the last years of its external course validation when it repeatedly encountered exciting innovations with real potential for improving the quality of student learning. These innovations, however, were related to conventional, inappropriate or inadequately thought through assessment methods which represented a real threat to standards and fairness or which actually undermined learning. The way in which assessment operates probably has more effect on student learning than any other aspect of course design. In many cases courses have dabbled with student centred teaching and learning methods only to be tripped up by problems with assessment and have reverted, chastened, to conventional techniques. For example, a large business school banned the use of all group work after embarrassing and justified appeals from students because of the unfair way group project marks were allocated to individuals.

'Assessment methods for student centred courses' was designed to analyse the nature of problems faced by the various forms of assessment used on student centred courses and to locate and describe examples of good practice which overcame these problems in imaginative and rigorous ways and which others could usefully emulate.

A team of eight consultants was formed. They met in order to analyse what 'student centred' really meant, to list the types of assessment which were being introduced in student centred courses and to research and analyse each of these forms of assessment. The team sought out case studies of best practice in their own institutions. This proved harder than envisaged. Some institutions proved to be more fruitful sources of cases than others and one University was unable to produce a single usable case study. The team had to use a wider range of institutions than originally planned. While a relatively large number of cases was eventually identified and preliminary descriptions produced, few cases satisfactorily tackled all the key problems. It became clear that even where lecturers were proud of their innovations, and had sometimes published accounts of them in order to share their achievements, the innovations themselves often left serious problems unaddressed.

The short case studies selected to be used in this book all contain worthwhile features which others can learn from. They address more problems than most. However, it is clear that there is still a considerable way to go before an assessment of student centred courses can be generally undertaken in a rigorous, rational and acceptable way. Of course many conventional assessment methods are also open to fundamental criticism concerning criteria, standards and fairness, but innovations are usually required to jump higher hurdles than existing practice!

One obvious omission here is the looming issue of assessment of NVQs and GNVQs in higher education. If and when higher level NVQs become widely assessed in Universities this will pose new challenges which go beyond the scope of the chapters here on assessing skills and competencies and on using profiles and which are different from those posed by the assessment of lower level NVQs in Further Education. Much good assessment practice in Higher Education has initially developed within BTEC courses and it may be that in future there will be new sources of insight and good practice associated with NVQs. This volume is however case based and there is at present too little relevant NVQ practice to draw conclusions from.

This book has been written in order to raise issues about the assessment of student centred courses and to provide checklists of questions which teachers can consult to review and improve their assessment practices. Course approval and review committees, those involved in course validation, and external examiners and quality assessors, can also use it as a handbook for reviewing others' assessment arrangements.

I would like to acknowledge the inspiration and hard work of the project team: Mike Carr, University of Oxford; Jessica Clarridge, University of Exeter; Diana Eastcott, University of Central England; Trevor Habeshaw, Technical and Educational Services Ltd; Haydn Mathias, University of Southampton; Liz McDowell, University of Northumbria; Fred Percival, Napier University; and Chris Rust, Oxford Brookes University. I would like to thank Alan Jenkins, Shirley Earl and Jennifer FitzGerald who wrote additional case studies, and Peter Griffiths and Mark Lejk for their cases. I would like to acknowledge the contribution of all those whose innovations are described in the case studies. Finally I would like to thank Sally Brown for her valuable and encouraging comments on my drafts.

1 Introduction: Definitions, Problems and Key Features

Definitions and rationales

There has been a major shift in patterns of teaching in British Higher Education towards more student centred methods. Assessment patterns have been transformed, with an enormous increase in the contribution to students' qualifications of progressively more student centred coursework assessment. By student centred is meant courses where the emphasis is on:

- learner activity rather than passivity, and what the student does in order to learn rather than on what the lecturer does in order to teach;

- students' experience on the course, outside the institution and prior to the course, rather than on knowledge alone;

- process and competence, on how students do things, rather than just on content and what they know;

- and, most importantly, where the key decisions about learning are made by the student, or by the student through negotiation with the teacher, rather than solely by the teacher. These decisions include:

  - what is to be learnt (the goals);

  - how and when it is to be learnt (the methods and schedule);

  - with what outcome (the assessment product or evidence);

  - what criteria and standards are used to assess the outcome;

  - what judgments are made (the marks or grades);

  - by whom these judgments are made.

A wide range of different movements employ an enormous diversity of student centred methods with a bewildering diversity of rationales. For example, learning contracts were initially developed to tap adults' motivation to learn. The Enterprise in Higher Education programme has concentrated on the development of transferable skills but also encouraged course processes which give students wider experiences and more scope for individual or collective initiative. Courses operating under the aegis of professional bodies (such as the Law Society's Legal Practice Course) are starting to adopt competency-based rationales in order to assure professional standards. Medicine has embraced more flexible course processes such as problem-based learning, not in order to negotiate objectives but as an effective way of achieving specified goals. And recently 'student centredness' has been sold as a solution to large-class problems. If students can be more independent, it is argued, then maybe they won't need so much of their teachers' time.

Underlying much of the adoption of student centred methods has been a concern that traditional teacher centred methods and syllabus centred methods have not always led to quality in learning but to passive, bored students giving back to teachers what they have been given in a worthless grade-grubbing way irrelevant to their future lives. There is no consistent rationale for student centred alternatives and no consistent pattern of implementation, and this is inevitable. But it also leads to a lack of clear definition and much confusion. This confusion is particularly evident in the assessment of student centred courses.

This publication is designed to bring a little more rigour and rationality into the sometimes reckless adoption of student centred assessment methods in order to help secure the future of student centred courses. To do this it is important to be realistic about the extensive range of problems these assessment methods face. Chapters 2 to 9 each examine a distinctive assessment method or clusters of related methods. The analysis of problems below applies to all of them.

Problems faced by student centred assessment

Changes in goals

Conventional assessment methods characteristically assess different outcomes to those assessment methods which are associated with student centred courses: for example, the ability to recall information or to tackle familiar forms of academic problems compared with the ability to identify and tackle new and unfamiliar 'real world' problems. Learning may be enhanced by the new course methods but this may not become apparent in results from conventional assessment methods. For example, students in a team who have pursued their own goals and undertaken team project work of personal significance to a high standard might perform poorly in an unseen exam designed to assess a pre-specified syllabus. This could easily be interpreted as a fall in standards and it takes careful research to reveal what is actually going on. To give another example, students having undertaken problem based learning in medicine, although they can be outscored by conventionally taught students on conventional tests of recall immediately after studying, score very considerably better as little as two months later. The student centred learning process here produces very worthwhile long-term benefits about which conventional assessment gives completely misleading evidence.

Even more seriously, the lack of congruence between course methods and assessment may actually undermine standards where students pay more attention to perceived assessment demands than to learning tasks. For example, students may bail out of their project team in order to revise for an exam, thus completely undermining their learning. The lack of congruence of goals and assessment is often a problem on conventional courses but it can be particularly problematic on student centred courses, especially where goals have not been clearly specified.

Worries about standards

Evidence from the extensive modular course at Oxford Brookes University shows that average marks on modules with significant amounts of coursework assessment are significantly higher than on modules with mainly unseen exams. Subject areas whose modules involve high proportions of coursework award a greater, proportion of good degrees than subject areas with low proportions of coursework. And many of the subject areas with higher proportions of coursework are new: Health Studies and Tourism, for example, have little tradition of academic standards, and use new assessment methods such as negotiated learning contracts and group projects. Group project work almost always produces higher marks than individual project work. Some would argue that this shows a fall in standards while others would claim that it shows improvements in the quality of what has been learnt.

Some of the difficulties relating to standards concern lack of familiarity with new methods. If a Humanities Department has always used essays for assessment or a Science Department has always used a particular form of laboratory report then a largely implicit shared sense of absolute standards will have developed over time between lecturers. The experience of differences in grades between courses, and informal discussion between lecturers, will have resulted in a shared sense of what an 'A' or a 'C' looks like. A new lecturer joining such a department would soon realise the need to adapt to these implicit standards. However, these standards tend not to be based on a clear rationale, stated objectives or any explicit criteria, but are usually simply the result of long familiarity and pragmatism.

In this situation almost any new form of assessment will face problems. Many of the traditional implicit criteria will have been related to teacher centred values (such as relevance to the set question or coverage of the syllabus) or features of the assessment task (such as characteristics of 'good' essay writing). Any student centred form of assessment will embody different values (such as originality or personal relevance) and is likely to employ forms of evidence of learning with very different features (such as portfolios or logs). There will be little shared experience of what quality consists of with such new methods, what standards should consist of, and how judgments about standards should relate to degree classifications. So new standards have to be established – usually by being explicit about the underlying rationale and values, by stating objectives, learning outcomes or competencies, and by specifying criteria and the way they relate to marks or grades. It is impossible to resolve the question of whether standards are being maintained with new assessment methods if there is no explicit definitions of standards for either old or new methods.

Students are even more unfamiliar with new assessment methods than teachers and if they are to be involved in assessment their judgment also needs to be sharpened. Peer assessment of seminar presentations commonly produces high marks. This is not, however, inevitable, and could be changed by training students to use explicit criteria more carefully.

Reliability

New lecturers tend to be unreliable in their marking simply through lack of experience and many new assessment systems turn experienced lecturers temporarily into novices.

Marking of open-ended assessment tasks such as essays or projects is often very unreliable, despite lecturers' confidence that they can reliably distinguish between a high 2:2 and a low 2:1. For example, a study of double marking of psychology essays at the University of Cambridge found no significant correlations between markers: marks were effectively random. A study of internal and external markers of psychology assignments at the University of Plymouth found marks for a script varying by up to 35% between markers and external examiners to be even less reliable than internal double markers.

Many student centred assessments are inherently open-ended and there is little precedent or experience to draw on. Very low reliability should be expected unless careful steps are taken.

Averages and grade distributions

From experience, lecturers learn to calibrate their assessment systems so as to produce an 'acceptable' distribution of 1sts, 2:1s, 2:2s, 3rds and Fails. They achieve this by a judicious mixture of adjusting the size of the syllabus, the number and difficulty of the assessment questions or tasks, the predictability of these questions, and, finally, by implicit criteria for allocating grades or marks.

When new assessment systems are used this calibration is often askew, producing an unacceptable distribution of grades. It may be that features of student centred courses actually succeed in producing better learning outcomes, but lecturers are not usually permitted to report anything other than a 'normal distribution' of grades. Many features of student centred courses can disrupt the expected distribution of grades. For example, if objectives and criteria are clarified, students are less likely to completely miss the target and score very poorly. With 'criterion referenced' assessment, such as that involved in competence-based profiling, for example, it is theoretically possible for all students to achieve 100% by demonstrating all the competencies on the list, which would be impossible with 'norm-referenced' assessment. Students in teams produce better products than individuals and project work often produces more commitment and higher quality results than do conventional exams. Teamwork, by averaging to some extent the abilities of students within teams, also tends to produce less variation between groups than is usually experienced between individuals. Unless special steps are taken, team project work therefore tends to produce an unacceptably high average and an unacceptably low spread of marks.

Many aspects of student centred assessment can distort averages and grade distributions. In time, it will be possible to calibrate the extent and difficulty of new assessment tasks and to sharpen criteria and marking schemes in order to spread the grade distributions out again, but if initial problems are too severe then this time may not be given.

Validity

There are features of essays (or science problems) which lecturers assume embody what academic study of the discipline is all about: evidence of particular forms of scholarship, rational thought, rigorous use of established techniques, or whatever. This is usually 'face' validity rather than that established by careful task analysis or supported by evidence of similar student performance on related academic tasks. Lecturers, however, believe in this validity. What is actually being measured when a student submits a diary for assessment may be less clear and convincing. What features of scholarship are embodied in students' assessments of each others' seminar presentations may not at first be apparent. Student centred assessments need to justify their validity and demonstrate it through careful task analysis and evidence of correlations with student performance on the 'real world' tasks the assessment tasks are meant to simulate or prepare students for.

Proof of authorship

Unseen exams are probably the safest form of assessment if plagiarism or cheating is suspected. As soon as coursework is assessed the possibility arises of students gaining outside help or taking material from other sources and presenting it as their own. Most student centred courses involve assessment methods where there is more scope for this kind of dishonesty and some forms, such as those which encourage co-operation and teamwork, may make it impossible to identify an individual's contribution.

Students' focus of attention

Student centred courses may be designed to engage students and to both deepen and broaden their learning. However, the courses also often involve bringing learning and assessment closer together (as with learning contracts or project work). This can have the effect of limiting learning to those areas which will be assessed. As student centred assessment is often more explicit and predictable, students may learn little beyond the negotiated contract or set project. Students in group project work may even concentrate only on their sub-task within the group task. Conversely, it is sometimes argued that the only way to give students freedom to learn is to completely separate assessment from learning – as with unseen final exams. It is obviously a matter of dispute whether conventional exams broaden or narrow student learning but it is often equally unclear whether student centred methods are better or worse than such exams. If 'coverage' of a curriculum is important this may rule out a wide range of student centred methods.

Levels of dispute

Despite low levels of popularity with students, conventional teacher-centred assessment methods often lead to low levels of dispute. This may only be because the system of marking is such a mystery, and conventional assessment systems so shrouded in secrecy, that students have no grounds for dispute. It is common for students not to be given their coursework marks, informed only of broad grades rather than marks, not to have their projects returned, and certainly not to have their exam scripts returned with detailed justification of their marks. In contrast, student centred methods tend to be more open and transparent. It is therefore easier for students to see where there might be inconsistencies of standards or even errors in marking, resulting in plenty of scope for dispute. Where the judgment of fellow students is involved this can exacerbate the situation. It is sometimes assumed that student centred methods somehow obviate the necessity for teacher control or rules but there is often a need for greater specification of ground rules and regulations when these methods are used.

Levels of acceptability

While students may dislike essays or problem questions in exams, they tend to think these methods are fair, and they are probably familiar with their format. There are many features of student centred assessment which can initially give rise to objections from students. While students largely trust the judgment of their lecturers they may not trust the judgment of their peers in peer-assessment. While they may be happy to be judged as an individual they may be unhappy to be judged as a member of a team containing weaker students. While they may be happy being judged on writing a lab report with which they are familiar, they may feel insecure about being judged on writing in a form they are unfamiliar with, such as a personal account or a log. Students' lack of familiarity with student centred assessment methods, lack of clarity of task demands and lack of confidence in their own and their peers' judgment often leads to low levels of acceptability. This can usually be overcome by sensitive design and careful introduction and explanation and students can get to accept and trust very radical approaches. However, low levels of initial acceptability can kill a course, especially where standard student feedback questionnaires based on conventional assumptions are used.

Unintended side effects

All assessment systems have unintended side effects. Courses assessed by unseen exams encourage question-spotting and selective negligence. Courses involving frequent assessed laboratory reports leave students with little time to read. Courses with set problems and tests can discourage exploration or diversity, and so on. Student centred courses and their assessment systems produce their own unintended side effects. Teamwork may stifle individual interests. Learning contracts may set objectives too early and discourage the development of ideas and goals. Fixed criteria or profiles may undervalue unusual or unpredicted qualities or competence. There is usually a trade off between different goals and when different methods are adopted it is not always easy to anticipate when some of one's treasured values are traded-off against new goals. For example, student engagement and motivation may be achieved at the expense of rigour or of familiarity with the full range of fundamentals of one's discipline

Volume

Assessing coursework usually involves increasing the volume of marking. Many student centred courses where assessment has moved closer to learning activities involves a great deal of marking. With increased student numbers and a decline in resources per student this often puts an intolerable strain on lecturers, especially where double marking is required. This is often resolved either by reverting to cheaper traditional methods or by doing it in a rush. It is an almost universal experience that students' work is receiving less careful attention, and this can reduce reliability of marking as well as quantity and quality of feedback. An alternative is to separate the formative functions of assessment which support learning from the summative function of measuring learning outcomes, and to free much of the assessment from the burden of producing trustworthy marks. The volume of learning activity can be maintained by making assignments course requirements, and feedback can be maintained – or even increased – if peer assessment is used (in a way which does not contribute to marks). Sometimes the key to making student centred assessment work with inadequate resources is to stop trying to obtain marks from it.

Key features of successful assessment systems

Clear rationale

The reasons for introducing a student centred course and the associated assessment methods should be well thought through, consistent and explicit. Decision making about details of the operation of the assessment, for example whether students should have choice over project topics, should be guided by a rationale for the course, not just a general commitment to student centred learning. I have seen a course with specified learning outcomes involving a list of competencies to be acquired by every individual student adopt group assessment 'because students learn well in groups' despite the difficulty of assessing an individual's competencies through group assessment. Group work might or might not have supported the acquisition of the competencies but an individual form of assessment would have been more appropriate. I have seen individually negotiated project work used on courses where coverage of a full range of topics is necessary 'because students learn best when they decide what they want to learn' but where project work would have led to most of these topics being ignored and there was, in reality, little scope for student choice. If a number of tutors work in parallel to implement a course it is crucial that they understand and are committed to the same rationale.

Explicit values, aims, criteria and standards

Where course and assessment design decisions are guided by values, these need to be made explicit to students. If it is believed that students will only learn to tackle messy real world problems by practice with messy real world problems, then this should be explained. If graduates find themselves working co-operatively in teams and you believe that too much of education is solitary and competitive then you should explain this in introducing team work. If the aims of the use of portfolios is really to make sure students work evenly across all elements of the course then students should know this, and also know why you think it is important. If there are criteria for assessment it is vital that students know what they are, understand what they mean and can apply them to their own work. If there are clear standards (to get an "A" you would need to do X and if you do Y you will fail) then it is vital these are explicit so that students have a clear target to aim at or at least a sound basis for making decisions about their own studying. Students need to be on the inside of the logic of the course, believing in its rationale, not tagging along, feeling bewildered and jumping through hoops.

Effective induction

Many of the methods described in Chapters 2 to 9 will be new to students and involve new skills. Just as essay writing involves skills without which it is difficult for students to demonstrate their learning, so negotiating a contract, keeping a reflective diary, or working in groups, involve skills without which it may be difficult to learn and what has been learnt may be invisible. Induction means more than a quick exercise or a briefing. It may be sensible to have a 'dry run' at group work or peer assessment of seminar presentations, learning to use new methods, applying new criteria and so on before the first time that marks are awarded and count. It may be necessary to plan the gradual introduction of methods: for example, a short group task with no assessment in a year 1 module, a longer group task counting for 25% of marks and introducing team skills and peer feedback which does not contribute to marks, in year 2, before embarking on a full-blown extended group project based module with peer assessment of team members' contributions in year 3. Students will need time to reflect on the way these methods operate – discussing them with peers and even writing up their experiences, as part of learning how to make them function. It is students who make student centred methods work, not tutors, and they cannot manage this if they do not know how to.

A facilitative degree of structure

Students need just that degree of structure, and of freedom, which is optimally helpful. This does not mean that absolutely everything should be decided by students or negotiable, or that everything should be self assessed, or that if students want to make a video instead of writing a project report this is automatically OK. One of the most common failings of student centred courses is that there is more flexibility than students can handle and too little structure to guide and focus work towards useful learning outcomes. Some of the most effective student centred courses I have ever encountered involved entirely specified learning outcomes and tutor set and marked assignments with all the students' attention focussed around using the flexibility that existed in getting to the specified end points effectively. It can help students to work out their own criteria for the assessment of a group assignment, although not necessarily the first time they encounter group work. They may initially have their hands full learning to work as a group and would greatly appreciate the criteria being fixed and the lecturer doing the assessment until they have got some of the other components under control. It is usually desirable to work towards more 'pure' forms of student centred courses and assessment gradually, over time, and it is usually helpful to introduce responsibility and freedom in manageable stages.

Assessment which drives student learning appropriately

Assessment should operate in ways which support the student centred learning the course is designed to produce. As an example, a Financial Accounting course at London Guildhall University wanted students to work co-operatively in 'learning sets' which involved peer tutoring and mutual support. However, there was a two hour closed book examination. In its conventional form this could have resulted in students working in isolation and competitively and would have undermined the operation of the learning sets. To support the process more appropriately students were told that instead of receiving their own mark in the exam they would receive the average of the marks of the members of their learning set. The result was that the members of the sets worked co-operatively on examples, sharing a desire that everyone got the answers right and understood the concepts rather than that only one person had got it right. It improved average marks on the exam from 46% to 60%. Even after the exam learning set members offered assistance to those who had failed and needed to re-sit, and did so because the re-sit mark was allowed to be substituted, a higher re-sit mark thus benefiting everyone in the set (Cooper, 1994). There is no guarantee that assessing the products of co-operative group work (for example a group project report) would have produced such uniformly high performance even if the examination regulations would have allowed it or appropriate group tasks could have been set. It is quite common either for conventional assessment to undermine student centred processes or for inappropriate student centred assessment to produce inappropriate student learning behaviour.

Safeguards

Conventional assessment involves exam regulations, deadlines, penalties for lateness, rules about copying other students' work and plagiarism, appeals procedures, and so on. These regulations have been built up through experience to safeguard both students and teachers. Sometimes new methods are introduced without any such safeguards either through oversight or through a misguided belief that student centred methods should not have such legalistic constraints. However, they are probably even more necessary with student centred methods and the more open-ended and flexible the methods the clearer these safeguards need to be. What is to stop students giving themselves over-high marks when using self-assessment, or a student from devising aims for a negotiated project which are too easy to achieve, or a student appealing against a mark for a very short portfolio on the grounds that its length was not specified in advance or an individual from refusing to contribute to a group task or a peer assessment exercise? Just as criteria and standards for conventional assessment come from familiarity and implicit agreement rather than explicit statements, so often do ground rules. In contrast there may need to be very explicit ground rules and safeguards for student centred methods and students' attention will need to be drawn to these ground rules.

Rigour

The introduction of student centred methods should be undertaken in a rigorous way involving collecting evidence that the methods are reliable, valid and fair and that problems have been overcome. If self assessment were introduced it would be vital that the reliability of self assessment marks was established, as well as their impact on student performance. If peer assessment of seminar presentations were introduced with criteria and rating scales it would be vital to see whether students used the scales in a discriminating way, producing marks with a reasonable mean and range, and that any systematic bias or unfairness was identified and eliminated. If project work were introduced on the assumption that it would increase student motivation then it would be vital that evidence was sought about student workload and attitudes. Too often self assessment methods are introduced with a touching but misplaced faith that improvements in the quality in student learning will be automatic and sufficient to outweigh any other problems which might emerge.

It is difficult to get things right first time and vital that development is informed by sound evidence. It is often necessary to defend oneself from attacks from those who believe in more conventional approaches and this is difficult to do without hard evidence.

Awareness of students' learning context

The design of assessment methods should take into account the other aspects of students' learning context outside the specific student centred course being assessed. Student centred methods are usually introduced by enthusiasts in quiet corners of courses, not as a wholesale policy across an entire degree. As a result there can be all sorts of problems for students operating in largely conventional contexts or within several completely different systems at once. They may normally be expected to do what they are told and follow instructions, to accept tutors' judgments as the only truth, and to take as few risks as possible in order to ensure reasonable marks. They may be used to doing little outside of class or only working on their own in competition with others. Criteria for essay marking on one module may be completely different from criteria for self-assessed project work on another. But it is not just a problem of incompatible values, goals and criteria. There can also be simple practical difficulties. A deadline for a project report may clash with revision time for conventional exams on a parallel module. A student may belong to a learning team which faces impossible logistical obstacles given the variety of differently timetabled modules the other team members are taking or even membership of other learning teams on other modules. Student centred courses and their associated assessment systems sometimes founder not because of any inherent flaw in otherwise well conceived designs, but because the context conflicts and disrupts so much.

Bibliography

Alverno College Faculty (1994), *Student Assessment-as-Learning at Alverno College,* 3rd edn, Milwaukee: Alverno College Institute

Andreson, L., P. Nightingale, D. Boud and D. Magin, eds, (1993), *Strategies for Assessing Students,* Staff and Educational Development Association Paper 78, Birmingham

Angelo, T. A. and K. P. Cross, (1993), *Classroom Assessment Techniques, A Handbook for College Teachers,* 2nd edn, San Francisco: Jossey-Bass

Boud, D. (1988), *Developing Student Autonomy in Learning,* 2nd edn, London: Kogan Page

Brown, G. and M. Pendlebury, (1992), *Assessing active learning,* Effective Learning and Teaching in Higher Education, Module 11 Part 2, Sheffield: CVCP

Brown, S. and P. Knight, (1994), *Assessing Learners in Higher Education,* London: Kogan Page

Brown, S., C. Rust and G. Gibbs, (1994), *Strategies for Diversifying Assessment,* Oxford: Oxford Centre for Staff Development

Cooper, K. (1994), *Group assessment using closed book exams,* Educational Developments 1,1, London: Guildhall University

Erwin, D. T. (1991), *Assessing student learning and development,* San Fransisco: Jossey Bass

Habeshaw, S., T. Habeshaw and G. Gibbs, (1993), *53 Interesting Ways to Assess your Students,* 3rd edn, Bristol: Technical and Educational Services

Mentkowski, M. and G. Loaker, (1985), 'Assessing and validating the outcomes of College', in P. Ewell, ed, Assessing educational outcomes, *New Directions for Institutional Research,* 47, pp. 47-64, San Fransisco: Jossey-Bass

Murray, J. P. (1990), 'Better testing for better learning.' *College Teaching,* 38, pp. 148-54

Nixon, N. J. (1990), 'Assessment issues in relation to experience based learning within courses', in C. Bell, ed, *World Yearbook of Education 1990: Assessment and Evaluation.* London: Kogan Page

Rowntree, D. (1977), *Assessing students: how shall we know them?* London: Harper and Row

Van Berkel, H. J. M. (1990), 'Assessment in a problem-based medical curriculum', *Higher Education,* 19, pp. 123-46

2 Assessing Group Work

Introduction

Group project work is one of the most common forms of student–centred learning. It is used for a wide variety of reasons:

- to increase the amount and quality of discussion between students and to foster informal peer tutoring and peer feedback;

- to enable students to be involved in larger-scale, more complex and more open-ended learning tasks than they could manage on their own;

- to produce better quality learning outcomes than any individual student could manage;

- to increase co-operation between students within groups, but with competition between groups, in order to produce maximum overall productivity;

- to develop students' team work skills but also to involve a whole range of other transferable skills, such as time and task management, creative problem solving and written and oral communication skills;

- to save resources. Group work can be more economical to set up, supervise, equip and mark than individually undertaken project work.

The main problem with group project work is that it is individuals who gain qualifications, not groups, and some way has to be found to allocate marks fairly to individuals. Simply allocating individuals the same group mark can lead to poor students benefiting from the work of better students (and vice versa, good students being brought down by poor students). Lazy or strategic students can opt out of their group without penalty. This can lead to justifiable resentment between students. If the group's product is not assessed, however, and individuals are only assessed using conventional methods such as an unseen exam, there is no incentive to take group project work seriously and students opt out in order to prepare for the exam. In addition, the effect of individuals efforts being averaged out within groups tends to produce a narrow overall range of marks, and, as group products tend to be better than individual products, higher means. As a consequence, without special additional assessment features the assessment of groups is normally considered thoroughly unsatisfactory.

Practical matters

There are a range of methods for overcoming the problems with group assessment.

Limiting the emphasis on the group mark

The problems outlined above may be considered tolerable provided that the group mark does not represent too large a proportion of the total mark for an individual for the course element being assessed – probably no more than 50% of the total marks available. In practice this often involves individuals contributing an individual report for assessment as well as a written group report or oral group presentation, or sitting an exam in addition to contributing to the group report. Some projects also involve diaries or logs which give the tutor evidence of a student's work throughout the group project which would not otherwise be open to inspection, and such logs can be assessed. The additional assessment may have to be designed carefully if it is not to involve excessive additional marking effort or to lead to students withdrawing their effort from the group work.

Judging students' relative contributions

On some courses tutors feel they have enough information about the way individual students have contributed to their group's work to be able to moderate the group mark to some extent for each individual. Usually the student starts off with the group's mark and the tutor moderates this mark up to about 10% either way for above or below average contributions. However, it is difficult for tutors to gain access to appropriate evidence. Observation of groups in action in class or during supervision sessions is difficult and time consuming and may provide little valid evidence concerning independent work outside class where most of the work gets done, and is highly subjective and open to personal bias. Diaries or logs may provide useful additional evidence. Vivas can also be used effectively where the size of the project justifies the time involved. It can be possible to judge an individual student's relative contribution to a group report with just a few well chosen questions in a brief viva.

Dividing up the group task

For some projects it may be possible to allocate different sub-elements of the group project to individuals and to allocate at least some of the marks to individuals for the element they were personally responsible for. However, it can be difficult to divide up projects into elements of equal size, difficulty or ease of marking – for example, background research and creative problem solving is less visible than oral presentation or report writing but may be equally important. Also, once students are responsible for separate components they may stop co-operating with each other in order to concentrate on their own piece of work. Fair marks for individuals may be achieved at the expense of good group work and a coherent project report.

Sharing the group grade

While the tutor may be in the best position to judge the quality of the product of the group work, the group may be in the best position to judge the relative contributions of its members. One way to use their knowledge is to allocate the group product a mark, multiply it by the number of students in the group, and then allow the group to decide for itself how this total should be divided between its members. Groups who have not thought about the implications of this in advance may contribute very unevenly but then opt out of the difficult decisions involved in allocating marks accordingly. It is therefore important to discuss how this process will operate at the outset and to discuss how students will go about dividing up the marks at the end. It can be helpful, the first time students experience such a process, to provide both criteria and a decision-making mechanism for students to use, rather than hoping they will come up with something appropriate and fair on their own.

Peer assessment of contributions

The use of clear criteria and rating scales can provide useful safeguards for the process of differentiating between the contributions of individuals. As described above, the tutor allocates a mark for the group product, but the students assess each others' contributions to a list of elements of the project – for example, to background research, data collection, design ideas, or whatever. It is possible to weight different elements according to their importance and to limit the overall impact of peer ratings on the extent to which individual marks will differ from the group mark. Again, explaining how everything works at the outset will both make it more likely to work at the end and to have a positive impact on group behaviour. A student who knows she/he will be peer assessed according to her relative contribution to the group's final presentation is unlikely to leave all the hard work to her/his colleagues.

Peer assessment of group process

It is possible to completely separate the assessment of content and process. Some courses leave all the assessment of the product to the tutor, with all students gaining their group's mark. But students then assess the way other individuals have worked in the group – their group work skills – rather than components of the product. The emphasis here is on process and the development of transferable skills and some sophisticated questionnaires and rating schemes have been developed, sometimes in conjunction with training for students in both recognising processes and skills and in giving feedback to peers.

Project exams

After a group project is over it is sometimes possible to set an exam question, under conventional examination conditions, to test individual student's knowledge and understanding of the work undertaken during the project. Such questions may only be able to be answered if the student was thoroughly involved in the group's work – indeed any other type of question will encourage students to bail out of their group in order to revise for the exam. Student's performance in this project exam can be used in addition to a mark for the group project, to moderate the group mark, or even instead of the group mark where examination regulations require the use of an exam.

Key Issues

The following issues may need to be addressed if the assessment of group project work is not to run into problems:

What are the aims of group work?

Is the quality of the product of group work most important, or does the process matter as well? And if the process is important, is it project work skills or group work skills which are most important? Assessment of group project work often runs into difficulties because it concentrates on aspects of the project work which were not of central importance to either the tutor or the students. The aims should be made explicit, and prioritised, before the assessment methods are designed and criteria agreed.

How big should the group be?

The larger the group, the more problems students will have co-operating and co-ordinating their efforts, the easier it is for students to 'hide' and the harder it can be to distinguish the contribution of individuals. Groups larger than six can lead to many problems and few benefits other than a saving in marking time and should not be used except deliberately to test students' ability to cope with complex group problems.

Should everyone in the group get the same marks?

If students are going to get the same marks as the other members of their group regardless of the quantity or quality of their contribution, then it is common for some to contribute little and concentrate on other aspects of the assessment system where their own effort has a more direct impact on their marks. Good students may resent being dragged down by poor students and poor students may unfairly ride on the ability of good students, even if they try hard. There are some circumstances in which everyone getting the same grade is appropriate – for example, where learning to function as a team is crucial and you want students to tackle the problems involved. However, normally one of the methods described above is required. Each of them will have different implications for student behaviour and even subtle differences in the ways these methods are introduced and operate can profoundly affect the quality of teamwork and of learning within a team. The crucial question is whether the way assessment works supports or undermines co-operative group learning.

How should groups be formed?

If groups are allowed to form themselves there will be groups of friends together. This will improve interaction and co-operation but may mitigate against rigour, self-discipline, or being able to tackle difficult group problems. There will also be groups of good students and a rump of poor students no group wants. This may open you up to accusations of unfairness. In work contexts teams seldom select their own membership and it may be more realistic to allocate students randomly. This will be perceived as more fair and will distribute stronger and weaker students more evenly. Allocating students on the basis of learning style, preferred group role or other quasi psychological grounds is difficult and unlikely to be very effective, though you may have good grounds for 'rigging' group membership to cope with individual idiosyncrasies you know about. If there is a succession of assessed group tasks it can be wise to change group membership from time to time so that there is no perception of unfairly carrying the same weaker student repeatedly or unfairly riding on the ability of a strong student repeatedly.

Does the group task require co-operation? How big and complex is the task?

Some group projects involve tasks which can simply be divided up and tackled separately by students who do not need to co-operate with each other. If you believe in the value of group work then the main tasks must require co-operation. Some tasks, although large and complex, are extremely difficult to co-operate on, such as extended essays. Some require both a large group, to cope with the size of the task, and sophisticated team work skills, to cope with the organisational complexity, and this will have implications for how much group experience students need and how prominent process variables become.

Are different groups working on the same task?

When different student groups are working on different tasks (for example sub-components of a very large task, or parallel tasks on related topics) it can be difficult to make the tasks of equal size and difficulty so as to ensure reasonable fairness. It can also be difficult to ensure that all groups learn similar things. This may not matter if there is no component to the assessment other than the product of group work. But if there is a later exam, or if the group work feeds in to later modules, then it makes a great deal of difference what each group tasks consists of. While it may appear to the lecturer that the whole syllabus has been covered, each group may only have covered a small part of it and this may leave different groups' members in a difficult position. If groups can negotiate the task then this can make it difficult for the tutor to calibrate the difficulty of different groups' tasks and make it very difficult to ensure that all groups have tasks which provide opportunities for all members to contribute, learn and gain credit equally. As with all student centred methods each additional layer of student centredness and flexibility brings with it additional potential problems.

17

Does everyone in each group benefit or learn the same?

Even if each group tackles the same task the individuals within groups may tackle different sub-tasks. What is to stop individual group members from avoiding the very content or skill they should be learning, such as using the computer, analysing the statistics, writing up the report, or from avoiding a group skill such as leadership? If one student tackles sub-topic A and another tackles sub-topic B, will either be disadvantaged in their learning or in subsequent assessments involving topics B or A? If group work is superimposed on a tight syllabus or fixed list of learning outcomes it is important to devise group tasks and processes in a way which enables each student to achieve every desired outcome and not just the one they choose to tackle. If this is not possible to arrange then group work should not be used.

Is the effectiveness of the group assessed?

If the purpose of the use of groups is to increase student learning on a particular topic rather than to develop group skills then it may not be appropriate to assess process as well as content. If skills are important, however, it will be necessary to specify criteria and to discuss what the group work skills are which are being assessed and what the criteria mean. Will the group be assessed as a group or will individuals be assessed according to their unique contribution to the group's effectiveness? What evidence will be used? As observation may be impossible or unrepresentative, courses normally rely on self-reporting, usually in writing, which may tell you more about students' reporting skills than about their group skills. If individuals within groups are assessed then this will mean relying on the ability of other students to recognise effective group behaviour when they see it. Those with good written reporting skills may not be the same as those with effective group leadership skills, and those performing low profile but vital group maintenance functions may be unfairly judged as less skilful than extroverts who are vocal but who may have few group skills. And what evidence of group effectiveness will external examiners see except the product of group work?

What fail-safe mechanisms are there?

Groups may collapse due to intractable personality clashes or illness of key members. Projects, especially those devised by students themselves, may turn out to be unmanageable in the time. Individuals may, for whatever reason, entirely fail to come up with the goods for their key part of an interlocking whole. Should everyone in the group suffer lower marks or even fail because of this? You may need ground rules to fall back on, just as there are examination rules in the eventuality of individual illness during final exams. With group work, however, the implications may be more far reaching. Most lecturers experience fewer disasters than they originally anticipate but it is reassuring for students to know what the fail-safe position is and this may reduce resistance. Some tutors allow themselves to intervene quite subjectively if they feel that an individual or group has been unfairly disadvantaged and students may find this reassuring or alarming depending on their trust in the tutor.

Are students involved in assessment?
It is very common when group work is assessed to involve students in peer assessment of other groups' work or in peer assessment within groups of other students' contributions. This is not necessary, however and should not be introduced without a specific purpose. It is sensible to separate assessment of the quality of products (which the tutor may be in the best position to judge) from assessment of process (which students may be in the best position to judge – though see above).

Do students understand the assessment from the start?
The way the assessment of groups works affects student behaviour right from the start – in choice of groups, in the degree of co-operation, competition and responsibility and so on. Having a well worked out system for dividing marks fairly will not have the desired effect if it is not introduced until after groups have submitted their work. It is vital that students understand exactly how marks will be allocated, right from the outset. This might mean students being involved in applying or even negotiating criteria, or hearing accounts from past students of how it works.

Where do students get the skills to work in groups?
Students who have never worked in groups before can struggle badly and can fail to produce anything worthwhile. I am not talking here about awareness of group dynamics or sophisticated group facilitation skills but the practical basics of getting a group task completed to a deadline: appointing a note-taker to record decisions, or setting a time for the next meeting. Students need to learn to undertake small tasks in small groups before tackling extended tasks in groups bigger than four and they need practical advice (cf. Gibbs, 1994a, 1994b) and opportunities to reflect on group experiences. Students deserve a trial run at unassessed group work before it is assessed in a way which contributes towards their degree and may also need trial runs at any peer assessment process involved. Even if the development of group skills is not a priority, a modest investment in developing such skills will improve student performance and make assessment of the products of group work fairer and more valid.

How is an appropriate distribution of marks achieved?
Groups tend to produce better work than individuals and so group work tends to produce higher average marks than individual work. Also the effect of putting mixed students together in groups is to make groups less varied than individuals – producing a narrower spread of marks between groups than between individuals. The common outcome is a high mean and a low standard deviation with no fails. If this is unacceptable then steps need to be

taken to manipulate grading in some way. Markers can adjust their standards subjectively over time (just as coursework marking needs to use different standards than exam marking to avoid much higher coursework marks than exam marks). Rating scales linked to criteria can be used which shift the mid-point in the scale downwards to change the relationship between judgments and marks. Any of the methods described above to allocate marks to individuals will have the effect of increasing variation between students and some (such as the use of project exams) will also reduce averages.

Are there intermediate deadlines?

As with extended project work, extended group work can benefit from intermediate deadlines and intermediate assessment – of plans, progress reports or drafts of final reports – as a way of guiding progress and keeping groups on track. An opportunity to review the operation of the group and compare it with others is also valuable before things go too wrong or in time to make productive changes to working practices.

Case Studies

Assessing team projects in Systems and Analysis Design

Graham Gibbs

Innovator: Mark Lejk, Computing, Sunderland University

A Structured Systems Analysis and Design module involves 250 students. Team projects are commonly four weeks long and involve four roughly equally difficult tasks. Students are usually allowed to select their teams of four for themselves, though as they use Belbin's team roles questionnaire they learn who might be useful team members and what combinations work well.

A number of consecutive tutorial sessions are scheduled and dedicated to the assignment. The first involves team building exercises: establishing ground rules for team behaviour and establishing strengths and weaknesses of team members. By the second tutorial the teams have to have completed any team building activities and identified who in the team is doing which task. By the end of week three all individual work has to be complete and distributed amongst the team members. They then peer review and improve these components before submitting both the individual work and the team design solution for marking.

70% of marks for each assignment are for the solutions to the tasks which have been set. Only the group's final work is assessed, not the individual work, which is submitted simply to show that each student has contributed. 30% of the marks are for a report on team building and team management. These reports contain:

- results of the use of the Belbin team roles questionnaire;

- the ground rules the team established for itself;

- details of discussions;

- project plans;

- individual work schedules;

- minutes of meetings;

- results of monitoring exercises

- a résumé of the team peer review exercise.

A single mark is awarded which the four students share. The safeguards for this process include:

- the team assignments only count for 25% of the module marks while 75% come from individual assignments and an examination;

- each individual within a team has an individual task and their work is submitted as evidence that they have completed this, even though it is not marked;

- teams are trained how to function and sort out their problems and a proportion of the marks is awarded for how well they have done this;

- in the last resort teams have powerful sanctions over recalcitrant members. They can award a 'yellow card' as a warning, which can reduce the individual's mark by 20% if the card is not rescinded, and a 'red card' if this warning is not heeded, which can result in the student receiving no marks at all. The use of the cards is mediated by the tutor and is described in formal procedures for the module:

   'If it becomes apparent to members of the team that one or more of the team members is or are not pulling their weight for various reasons, they can approach the tutor and ask that this member is awarded a YELLOW CARD! If the tutor agrees then the student is warned. It is possible for the team to ask the tutor to remove the yellow card later if there is sufficient improvement. If the team decides that the member does not deserve to have the yellow card removed then a deduction of 20% will be made for this student from the final team mark.

   If there is no improvement in the behaviour of a yellow card holder then the tutor can award a RED CARD. The student will then be excluded from the team and be awarded a mark of ZERO. The task(s) that were allocated to this student are then struck off the list and the rest of the team get on with the rest of the tasks.'

The students greatly welcome this potential sanction but, in practice, its existence is enough of a threat to produce appropriate team behaviour and very few yellow or red cards are ever issued.

This teamwork produced higher quality outcomes than individual work (due to the support, peer tutoring and operation of the assessment system) and very few problems with individuals. Marking was very similar to previously as the products of team work were relatively conventional in nature and involved no new criteria or problems.

Peer assessment of Group Problem-Solving and Group Writing

Shirley E. Earl, Educational Development Unit, The Robert Gordon University; Innes C. Hendry, School of Computer & Mathematical Sciences, The Robert Gordon University

Innovators: John Usher, Shirley Earl, Innes Hendry and 17 lecturers at The Robert Gordon University, Aberdeen

Course Context

Initial development of group work focussed on an applied modelling exercise in a Mathematical Models and Methods course in the second and third years of the Ordinary degree. Development was then extended to a major piece of project work which was the focal point of the Honours year, an 11-week Industrial Group Project.

The traditional methods of assessment on courses was by an individual, formal written examination. When courses began to embrace group activity general approaches to assessment remained static. The innovators, however, argued that an effective mathematical scientist must possess technical knowledge in the mathematical sciences and an ability to apply that knowledge in an industrial or commercial environment, and nowadays this means operating in interpersonal situations where group dynamics and communication skills are important and where employee performance is carefully monitored.

Peer assessment was therefore presented as being immediately relevant to the employment context, providing a comparison with self-appraisal and accessing areas of activity from which staff are excluded. As peer assessment of the modelling exercises has matured, peer assessment as a technique has gained credibility and, in various forms, has become part of other degree and diploma courses.

Description of Assessment

The work of a group is assessed by the supervising staff using three main categories for marking:

*   group activity;

*   oral presentation of results;

*   written report presentation.

Since it is impossible for supervisors to be aware of all the complex interactions which take place between group members, a peer-assessment scheme has been devised to take heed of student opinions of each other. The following describes the scheme and shows how marks for Group Activity and the Written Report are modified to incorporate information from peer assessment.

Marks for oral presentation given to any group are unmodified. All members keep this mark in common as a way of encouraging corporate responsibility.

Group Marking by Supervisors

Supervisors allocate marks on a scale of 0–10 for each of the three marking categories. A mark of 7.5 indicates 'very good', 8 would be 'excellent' and a mark of 10 has never been allocated! Towards the other end of the scale a mark of 4 is passable, below 4 is unsatisfactory.

Peer Assessment Scheme

Members of the groups are required to assess the other members of the group for their contribution to Group Activity and to Writing the Report. The Peer Assessment Scheme was devised after observing how staff in employment are assessed on performance, commonly on factors involving rating scales. It seemed logical to introduce similar scales for factors appropriate to the peer assessment and desirable in collaborative work and to use these to produce marks. The peer assessment forms are shown in Appendix A and Appendix B respectively. For Group Activity assessment ten skills are included and for Report Writing assessment, five skills. The rankings are added to give marks out of 50 and 25 respectively. For a group of four individuals the peer marks are further analysed in order to take into account the different performance of individuals within the group, as can be seen in the example for peer assessment of group activity in Table 1.

In Table 1 'Factor F' is defined as the individual mark divided by the group mark, and is a measure of the extent to which students have performed above or below the group mean. In the example in Table 1 students have produced very different marks for the four group members.

Incorporating Peer Assessment into the Final Marking Scheme

A typical piece of work might be allocated 35 marks, this could contribute 10% of a total course mark for the year, the total mark also including other coursework and an examination. In such a case the 35 marks would be subdivided into Activity/Oral/Report, out of 10, 10 and 15 marks respectively. The report marks therefore need to be weighted differentially.

Table 2 indicates the final marks obtained using the illustrations in Table 1 if the supervisor's group marks for Group, Oral and Writing were 6.0, 6.0 and 5.5 out of 10 respectively. As can be seen, the effect of this mathematical moderation is not very marked, but it is enough to get students to take their team roles seriously. Although the process looks complicated it is very easy to set up on a spreadsheet for automatic calculation of marks.

Table 1   Group 1 – Peer marks for activity

Mark given by	Mark given concerning				Group Average Mark
	Student A	Student B	Student C	Student D	
Student A	–	32	37	34	
Student B	45	–	44	41	
Student C	33	27	–	32	
Student D	36	25	40	–	
Total	114	84	121	107	
Average	38	28	40.3	35.7	35.5
Factor F•	1.07	0.79	1.14	1.01	

Table 2   Assessment summary

		Group Activity 10 marks		Oral 10 marks		Group written Report 15 marks		Student Mark 35 marks		100
Student	Group	Base Mark	Factor F	Indi Mark* M1	Common Base Mark M2	Base Mark	Factor F	Ind Mark** M3	M1 +M2 +M3	
A	1	6.0	1.07	6.4	6.0	5.5	1.00	8.3	20.7	59
B	1	6.0	0.79	4.7	6.0	5.5	1.08	8.9	19.6	56
C	1	6.0	1.14	6.8	6.0	5.5	0.88	7.3	20.1	57
D	1	6.0	1.01	6.1	6.0	5.5	1.04	8.6	20.7	59

*   Individual Mark =   Base Mark x 1.0 x F
**   Individual Mark =   Base Mark x 1.5 x F

Evaluation and Discussion

Over time the initial factors used have been modified by negotiation between students and staff. No requests for modification have been received since 1989.

Since the inception of the course there has been only one case in which a student's personality appeared to prohibit collaborative working in a group. The same student did not relate well generally to class peers and academic difficulties led to failure of his first attempt at year 2. A repeat of the year was achieved successfully by the student though his peer assessment marks have remained below the usual lowest values. As the student continued, his interactive skills and the situation improved.

Since the inception of the course, staff have observed a general pattern in student reaction to peer assessment. During year 2 students express doubts and worries. Throughout year 3 they are happy. As they approach year 4 there appears to be a qualitative leap in understanding the interactive mechanisms involved in problem-solving and report writing and in reasons for peer assessment. It was the students of the first Honours cohort who insisted on retaining peer assessment in the Industrial Group Project and during the subsequent years of the operation of the Honours degree external examiners have expressed concern on one occasion only.

The marks contributed to Honours classification and the external examiner was concerned that peer marking which could add or subtract up to 7% could cause unfair advantages or disadvantages. In practice, the sum of moderations has been extremely small, affecting final marks between 0.8% and 1.2%.

Appendix A: Peer Assessment of Group Activity Proforma

ROBERT GORDON UNIVERSITY
School of Computer and Mathematical Sciences

CONFIDENTIAL
PEER GROUP ASSESSMENT FORM

BSc in Mathematical Sciences with Computing - Mathematical Models and Methods

Please assess your GME colleague by giving a mark of 1-5 (by ticking the appropriate box) in each of the following ten categories.

NB This form will be treated in strict confidence

Name (of Colleague being assessed):

	5	4	3	2	1	
Regularly makes a useful contribution in group discussion						Finds it difficult to be a contributing group member
Can be relied upon to carry out allocated duties accurately and without supervision						Needs more supervision than most in carrying out instructions assigned to her/him
Works amicably with others as a member of a team						Has difficulty in working with colleagues and is sometimes not accepted as a member of the team
Responds well to instructions/advice/criticism						Resents criticism and is reluctant to accept advice
Is consistently courteous and helpful to colleagues						Appears off-hand and casual in dealing with colleagues
Shows excellent ability to plan and complete own work						Has not yet learned to organise own work effectively
Is outstanding in ability to organise and supervise work of others						Is not able to organise and supervise work of others
Grasps essentials very quickly						Has difficulty in recognising essentials
Successfully anticipates the requirements of new situations and takes appropriate action						Has difficulty in recognising implications of new situations
Is good at solving problem						Has difficulty in suggesting solutions to problems

Comments:

Your Name: **Date:**

Appendix B: Peer Assessment of Group Report Writing Proforma

ROBERT GORDON UNIVERSITY   **CONFIDENTIAL**
School of Computer and Mathematical Sciences   **PEER GROUP ASSESSMENT FORM**
                                                          WRITTEN REPORT

BSc in Mathematical Sciences with Computing - Mathematical Models and Methods

Please assess your GME colleague by giving a mark of 1-5 (by ticking the appropriate box) in each of the following five categories.

NB This form will be treated in strict confidence

Name (of Colleague being assessed):

	5	4	3	2	1	
Demonstrates awareness of the structure and presentation requirements of report writing						Seems unaware of the structure and presentation requirements of report writing
Shows excellent ability to plan and complete own elements of written team work						Has not yet learned to organise self as part of a writing team
Keeps colleagues informed about progress of the task						Appears casual in dealing with colleagues
Successfully anticipates requirements of a situation and takes appropriate action						Has difficulty in recognising implications of a situation
Is outstanding in ability to integrate and can amend and check written work						Is not able to integrate or amend and check written work

Comments: **Date:**

Your Name:

Bibliography

Cooper, K. (1994), Group assessment using closed book exams, *Educational Developments*, 1,1, London: Guildhall University

Earl, S. E. (1986), 'Staff and peer assessment: measuring an individual's contribution to group performance', *Assessment and Evaluator in Higher Education*, 11, pp. 60-9

Falchikov, N. (1988), 'Self and peer assessment of a group project designed to promote the skills of capability', *Programmed Learning and Educational Technology*, 25, pp. 327-39

Gibbs, G. (1994a), *Learning in Teams: A Student Guide*, Oxford: Oxford Centre for Staff Development

Gibbs, G. (1994b), *Learning in Teams: A Student Manual*, Oxford: Oxford Centre for Staff Development

Gibbs, G. (1995), *Learning in Teams: A Tutor Manual*, Oxford: Oxford Centre for Staff Development

Gibbs, G. (1992), *Assessing More Students* (Section 3.4: Assessing Students as Groups), Oxford: Oxford Centre for Staff Development

Goldfinch, J. and R. Raeside, (1990), 'Development of a peer assessment technique for obtaining individual marks on a group project', *Assessment and Evaluation in Higher Education*, 15, 3, pp. 210-31

Jenkins, A. and D. Pepper, (1988), *Developing Group Work and Communication Skills - A manual for teachers in higher education*, Birmingham: Standing Conference on Educational Development

Lejk, M. (1994), 'Team Assessment, Win or Lose', *The New Academic*, Summer, pp. 10-11

Thorley, L. and R. Gregory, (1994), *Using Group-based Learning in Higher Education*, London: Kogan Page

Usher, J. R. (1990), 'Development of a staff and peer assessment scheme for groupwork in mathematical modelling', *Teaching Mathematics and its Applications*, 9, pp. 1-5

Verran, J. (1993), 'Group Projects in Biological Science', *The New Academic*, 2, 2, pp. 9-11

3 Diaries, Logs and Journals

Introduction

Student diaries, logs and journals are often used in conjunction with other methods associated with experiential learning. They are used to:

* encourage and 'capture' reflection on experience and develop students' ability to learn through reflection;

* record learning activities and experiences, sometimes in conjunction with target setting, profiles or learning contracts;

* develop within students an awareness of personal response, such as an aesthetic response to art or an emotional response to a patient;

* provide evidence of engagemnent with a course and of the learning processes involved which would be hidden using conventional assessment products.

The terms diary, log and journal are often used interchangeably. For example, in 'A Guide To Learning Independently' (Marshall and Rowland, 1993), a section is entitled 'Keeping a journal/diary'. This section goes on to describe what a journal is and then has advice on 'Keeping a daily log'. The three terms are distinguished below in order to highlight the different types of use to which they are put and the different problems facing each when used as an assessment tool.

Practical matters

Diaries

Keeping a diary is often a very personal and private activity. The audience can be the diary itself (as in 'Dear Diary') or oneself rather than anyone else. It is often worked on regularly – perhaps every day or even more frequently. It may have very little structure other than headings identifying which day it is. It may never be shown to anyone else but if it is this may change how the diary is written - both in its content and tone. If it is assessed this will have a profound impact on what students write in their diary.

Diaries may be used by art history students while on a field trip as a way of recording their aesthetic response to objects of art they see, or by education students recording powerful emotions stirred up by difficult classroom experiences. Clinical psychology and counselling courses commonly use diaries as a way of encouraging self-analysis and gaining sufficient emotional distance to be able to reflect objectively on powerful direct experiences.

They may also be used in courses on writing, using the diary form as an easy way to start writing and as a source of ideas which feed into more formal assignments which are assessed.

Logs

A log may be simply a record of activities undertaken. In Music, students may be expected to keep a log of music they have listened to. In English Literature, students may be asked to keep a log of novels or poems they have read or plays they have seen or watched on television or video. In both Music and English, students are arriving in higher education with narrower experience than in the past and the requirement to keep a log may encourage students to be strategic in broadening that experience, noticing where gaps lie and seeking out opportunities to fill these gaps.

In creative subjects such as Architecture, students may be asked to keep a log as a record of the research they have undertaken or of other aspects of the process of design which would not otherwise be evident in the final product of a design project. This function may overlap with that of the portfolio (see chapter 9, Using Portfolios) where collections of draft designs are kept together in a folder.

In work-based learning, for example in nursing, teacher training or social work, students may be asked to keep a log of the jobs they have undertaken, the specific situations they have encountered, the skills they have used, the client groups or types of problems they have encountered and so on. Here the log can perform the function of a record-keeping system. The quantity and range of student experience recorded in the log may be assessed by matching it against course requirements for encountering a minimum range of situations or using a specified range of skills or competencies. This may involve using a profile (see chapter 8, Using Profiles).

In science, students may be expected to keep a log of their experimental work, practical classes or their fieldwork, rather than writing up full reports of every session. Such a log may be assessed for completeness rather than against criteria such as accuracy, neatness or conformity to report writing conventions.

Logs often involve the use of proforma, checklists, and formal and structured means of recording. They tend to be relatively impersonal and therefore easier than diaries to share and to assess. If the log includes reflection on experience it becomes a journal though logs may be used as a prompt for subsequent reflection in class, with other students, or in assignments.

Journals

Journals fill the middle ground between diaries and logs. They involve reflection, but not usually as private and personal in form as in diaries, and also records of activity or experience, but in a more reflective and analytical way than the record-keeping format of a log. They are much more likely to be summatively assessed than diaries and this can cause great difficulties (see below).

Training in writing

Most students are not used to keeping diaries or reflective journals and they need a considerable amount of help and support if they are to learn how to do this productively. They need clear guidance, examples, opportunities to see what other students write, the opportunity to experiment without risk, and time to develop a personal style of reflective writing which is both authentic and rigorous.

The first case study below involves tutors writing comments on students' journals in order to encourage and improve the quality of reflective writing: tutors do not assess them or even praise or criticise, but ask the kinds of questions which prompt further and deeper reflection.

Ground rules

Writing conventions for conventional assignments such as essays and reports are reasonably well understood and widely shared. The same cannot be said for diaries, logs and journals. Any ground rules, especially those affecting the acceptability of the writing for assessment purposes or assessment criteria, should be made explicit and discussion held to ensure that these ground rules are understood. For example:

- how long should a diary or journal be? Conventional essay or report lengths may be irrelevant but students need some yardstick;

- should writing be tidy or 'tidied up' or should everything, including rough and rejected work, be presented?

- should writing be in the first person, and chatty in tone, or do conventional academic conventions apply, including referencing?

- can writing be redrafted in the light of tutor feedback or discussion with other students, or must 'first drafts' be presented?

- is the writing saved up until a final deadline and assessed in one go or is it reviewed as the course progresses? Does this mean that all writing should be undertaken 'at the time' rather than retrospectively?

- are there categories of writing or topics which are expressly included or excluded? For example, should there be reflections on reading as well as reflections on experience? Should all personal reflection about the tutor, the tutor's colleagues, work colleagues or other students be excluded?

- is the writing confidential to the student and the student's tutor, or will others such as fellow students, other tutors or external examiners see it? In the second case study below the form of writing was formalised and confidentiality removed in order that the external examiner could see it.

Key Issues

Why are they used?

It should be absolutely clear to both the tutor and to the students whether diaries, logs and journals are being used primarily to support learning or to provide evidence of learning which can be used for assessment purposes. These are, to a greater extent than for other student centred assessment methods, incompatible goals. It should also be clear whether they are being used to structure experience, reflect on experience, or teach how to learn from experience. This third goal is addressed in the case study below concerned with developing trainee teachers as 'reflective practitioners'.

Can the same writing be both formatively and summatively assessed?

The key issues for diaries and journals is whether they can or should be summatively assessed to produce final marks at all. Diaries and journals are primarily designed to support learning through the reflection associated with writing. Formative assessment may involve tutors giving feedback designed to encourage further reflection, to check that students are continuing to write, and to develop students' ability to use these devices in order to learn. Any attempt to add marks to formative assessment will almost inevitably change the way students write, encouraging students to 'fake good' and 'please teacher' rather than writing for themselves. They will take fewer risks, be less revealing, less speculative, and turn the messy process of learning into a polished performance. This can easily undermine the potential value of diaries and journals. Summative assessment is less of an issue with logs, where students can be set explicit targets to meet (for example, for music students to listen to three new works a week) and where tutors may find it easy to check up on what students have or have not experienced or done. Where targets are less explicit or easy to check up on there will be a temptation for students to 'invent' experiences and log them and see the task as one of collecting ticks, rather than to use the log as a way of supervising themselves and seeking and recording experience. Even with logs it may be sensible to only require that the log is kept, relying on a separate assessment at the end which picks up the learning consequences of having used a log (for example, an exam or extended essay in music focussing on some of the music students have listened to and recorded in their log) rather than assessing the log itself. An exam question of the form: 'Analyse three contrasting experiences of X recorded in your log, using theoretical frameworks from the course' would encourage students to make sure that they had at least three experiences of 'X' recorded in their log, and had reflected on and analysed them. Summative assessment may be best undertaken completely separately, but in a way which supports the preceding student centred learning process.

There is also a problem if there has been formative assessment throughout the process of creating a diary or journal if it is later assessed summatively. To what extent has the tutor been responsible for the end product? It is common in PhD supervision for the supervisor not to be involved in the final assessment at all because of her or his close involvement in the development of the thesis. If there is final summative assessment it ought to involve, at the least, double marking and, ideally, totally independent marking.

Are the requirements clearly set up at the start? What is said to 'count' as diary entries?

Students commonly flounder the first time they are asked to write diaries or journals. They have great difficulty imagining what kinds of writing are acceptable and are very hesitant about committing pen to paper. It is a frequent experience that a proportion of students do not start at all for many weeks. It can be enormously helpful to have clear guidelines, tutor-generated examples and in particular, to see examples of 'acceptable' writing which models what you are after. This may involve informal sharing and feedback between students (with appropriate ground rules about confidentiality) early on, using samples from a previous year or from another source. 'The New Diary' (Rainer, 1980) contains many diary extracts which illustrate authentic reflection through writing and exercises and advice on how to use a diary effectively.

What effects do diary writing have on student learning and are these effects congruent with the aims of the course?

Diary writing is usually informal and personal but other writing, for example in essays and exams, is usually formal and impersonal. Students may normally be discouraged from drawing on personal experience, being criticised for being 'anecdotal', and encouraged to keep to a set syllabus rather than to pursue personal interests. The values associated with diaries and journals often clash with those of conventional courses and it may be important to be clear about how much you want the study behaviours associated with these values to spread over into other areas. This is particularly important where conventional assessment is retained alongside the use of diaries and logs.

What criteria are used for marking? What values inform criteria and judgments?

When marking a log it can be relatively straightforward to allocate marks for prescribed elements being present: five marks for a completed lab report, five marks for a literature review, one mark for evidence of each of the following experiences, and so on. Marking diaries is much more difficult. Is quantity valued over quality? Is objectivity valued over subjectivity? Is creativity and divergence valued over coherence and coverage of a syllabus? Is sensitivity in response valued over rigorous analysis in reflection? Is the exploration of personal issues valued over the analysis of academic issues? Often both ends of all these dimensions are valued but they can be mutually exclusive – a diary cannot be everything at once. Specifying the underlying values and the way they carry through into marking criteria is crucial if students are to understand what kind of diary they are being asked to write and if they are to find the assessment fair.

What counts as evidence of quality in reflection?

Even if criteria are clear it may not be obvious what kinds of writing would meet the criteria. A log of reading might list articles or books which had been referred to, but would that indicate anything about the quality of engagement with the reading? Would it be necessary to write reflective commentaries, and if so, how detailed and lengthy should these be? Would writing about reading which is linked to reflections about practice (for example a trainee teacher using literature to illuminate a classroom experience) count as better quality reflection than a wholly academic (but sophisticated) analysis of a book? I once encountered an Education course where, once students had spotted how the tutors judged 'quality of engagement with the material' quickly learnt to fake it, without the tutors realising. Although mastering such faking is not a trivial skill it was not exactly what was intended!

Is the diary kept up regularly or only after periods or at the end? How do assessors know?

It may be necessary to write within twenty-four hours, at the maximum, of an experience if details of personal experience are to be captured for subsequent reflection and analysis. If a log simply records what tasks have been completed it may be perfectly acceptable to keep it up-to-date each week. It is easy for students to fall behind and find themselves reconstructing their experiences in retrospect – even right at the end of a course. This is neither authentic reflection nor likely to lead to appropriate learning, but could a tutor tell the difference? It may be necessary to collect in diaries and journals at regular intervals, not to mark them but simply to ensure that they are being maintained.

Is there formative assessment?

If students receive no formative feedback on their writing they are very unlikely to produce the kind of end-product intended. Some of the most successful implementations of diary and journal writing involve regular and rapid feedback from tutors. Some courses return diaries with comments within twenty-four hours once every week to start off with. The function of this feedback should be purely to improve the quality of future writing and not to allocate marks. It should concentrate on questions to elicit further reflection and should limit judgments to re-orienting misconceptions of the purpose of the task. Such feedback can transform student writing and turn the mechanical and superficial meeting of requirements into a personal odyssey.

Giving this kind of feedback is not what tutors normally do and some are better at it than others. Those students with experienced and sensitive tutors will produce much better diaries than those whose tutors correct errors. If these diaries are then assessed the students with the best tutors will benefit unfairly. If several tutors are involved in the introduction of such reflective writing there should be mechanisms in place for tutors to compare the kinds of formative feedback they are giving and to discuss the ways their students are writing and how they are hoping they will write so as to standardise approaches within reasonable limits.

With logs it may be sensible to have an intermediate formative assessment in order to identify those things which students have not yet logged and experiences which they have not yet encountered so as to encourage the setting of learning targets.

Case Studies

Using journals and logs on a problem-based course in Engineering

Graham Gibbs

Innovator: Peter Griffiths, Mechanical Engineering, Coventry University

Course Context

The BEng Automotive Engineering Design at Coventry University involves a conventionally taught first year and a problem-based second and final years. The problem-based course has expanded rapidly in terms of the numbers of students choosing it and its methods have spread to other courses. It uses both journals and logs. Journals are used to help students to reflect on the way they are learning engineering. Logs are used as a record of work and contribute to assessment, illuminating how design projects have been undertaken.

Journals

The problem-based process involved is completely different from students' conventional first-year experiences and it is believed that reflecting on their learning will help them to adjust and to learn how to make the most of the course. Students are introduced to the experiential learning cycle through the use of a communications skills exercise and the Kolb experiential learning styles inventory. The role of reflection in learning is emphasised and students are then asked to make regular reflective notes about how they are finding the process of learning through problem solving: what they find different, difficult, intriguing or surprising. Tutors make formative comments on these journals and they are assessed as part of the 'professional skills' element of the course against clearly defined criteria. Their comments are intended to encourage more and better reflection. The following extract illustrates the kinds of things students write and also the way the tutor responded:

Student: '. . . it highlighted one of my problems that I have had for a long time – careless mistakes . . . I could not get the values to work out. It took me 20 minutes to find out that I hadn't square rooted to find their magnitudes. I don't feel this happened because I was distracted or not concentrating, as this kind of mistake has happened on many previous occasions. The problem perhaps lies in the speed at which I attack problems. Rushing things would perhaps cause me to miss the obvious . . . I have got used to rushing them. I will try in future to study the problem and the process involved more slowly and not to take it for granted the first thing that arrives in my head.'

Tutor: *'Very good reflecting . . .There is a tendency to rush at things. It is developed by the exam system. Answers are needed quickly. On this course you need to develop understanding as you go along. Plan your way through, getting the concepts clear. Number crunching must be accurate but modelling correctly is the key.'*

While the journals are largely private, the course leader reads other tutors' comments and helps them to learn to respond appropriately and uses journals in class from time to time to help discussion of how the students are getting on with their learning. Nevertheless, the style of writing students engage in clearly shows that they know their journals will be read, commented on and marked. Inevitably there is also some informal assessment going on here which will feed into tutors' judgments of students' other work, including the students' logs.

Logs

The logs are kept as a record of the work students have done while working on the problems and projects which make up the bulk of the course. Students are discouraged from tidying up their notes and instead present them 'warts and all'. Students are expected to reveal their level of understanding through their work records, explaining their mistakes, their strategies for sorting these out and their solutions, and it is this evidence of understanding which is assessed. Students are also interviewed about their design solutions, using their logs as a way of prompting questions and exploring students' understanding of their design decisions. There are no conventional exams and the course is assessed by 100% coursework.

The following written extracts from a student's log (without the accompanying diagrams and calculations) and the tutor's comments, illustrate the difference between the use of a journal and a log in this course. These log entries are about the content of the course and reveal the student's understanding of the key concepts involved and the way he has gone about tackling a problem.

Student: *'From the first part of the analysis . . . it was found out that the position of the nodes was critical. It was not sufficient to measure the nodes off the drawings. It was far more accurate to calculate them.'*

Tutor: *'The student here is drawing conclusions from a piece of work, comparing graphical and mathematical methods for performing the same function against criteria set by the particular circumstance of the project in hand.'*

Student: *'The problem is the following: the system is not symmetrical about the axis of the trailer. Therefore, if one side is located correctly, the other will be deficient.'*

Tutor: *'The student here is generalising and drawing principles from an experience which he will be able to use intuitively in future.'*

Student: *'The free body is wrong. It cannot be a simple rod submitted to two forces. There is a moment on each end of it not created by these two forces.'*

Tutor: *'The student here has made a hypothesis, tested it and found it wanting. On further analysis he is making a new hypothesis for how an element of his system is constrained to move which he is about to test. This is all discussed out in the open.'*

Such log entries are much more revealing than the tidied problem sheets which engineering students normally submit – tidied and sanitized, deliberately covering up the level of understanding involved.

This case illustrates the separation of formative tutor feedback on the process of learning, in students' journals, from summative tutor assessment of students' professional skills and of their logs which reveal their achievement of the objectives of the course.

Learning journals in a Women's Studies course

Jennifer FitzGerald, Queen's University Belfast

Innovator: Jennifer FitzGerald

Course Context

In 1992 a new course, 'Women, Culture, Texts' was mounted for an initial group of nine students. The course had a varied intake of students with mainly literary or sociological backgrounds. The course was largely assessed by essay but a 'learning journal' was also included for the first time. The use of a journal has been extended and formalised in subsequent years as student numbers have increased.

The journal

In 1992 students were introduced to the idea of a journal at the first meeting. Its objectives were stated as:

- to reflect on the experience of your learning on the course;

- to identify significant 'learning events' as they occur;

- to recognise how different 'learning events' are beginning to relate together as the course develops;

- to assess the role of your fellow students in the development of your learning;

- to assess any developments in your effectiveness in communicating; your capacity to solve problems, and the organisation and management of your learning;

- to assess your capacity for self-assessment;

- to reflect on your learning outside the class as well as inside.

Students were also given the following guidelines: 'You should spend a short time each week reviewing what has happened, how you have reacted, what you have done. In writing up your journal you might find it better to focus on one or two aspects of your learning experience each week, rather than to attempt a detailed and comprehensive account. To facilitate this process a series of prompt questions is attached. At two to three week intervals you should review what you have written and examine what pattern or development is revealed. The final item in your learning journal should review and comment on what you think is most significant in the body of the journal. Remember that your audience is in the first place yourself (and only secondly myself, as tutor). You may therefore wish to adopt an appropriately informal writing style.'

The tutor provided formative written feedback on the journals each week. Initially, students were confused about the purpose of the journals and what was expected and tended to write summaries of the content of class sessions. After four weeks it was neccessary to review the function of the journals and address the students' strong reactions. This changed some students' attitudes and approach. The uses to which the journal was put became more appropriate, though students continued to use it to record personal reactions to teaching and texts rather than to record 'learning incidents'.

Assessment

The journal initially counted for only 10% of the marks due to an examination regulation stating that student work which external examiners could not see could not contribute more than 10%, and the journal was confidential to the student and tutor. In the second year the journal assessment was formalised. A maximum length of 3000 words was specified and the journal became open to scrutiny by course tutors for monitoring purposes, by a second marker, and by the external examiner, allowing the assessment weighting to be increased to 25% but losing some of the confidential and personal tone. Longer and more detailed guidelines were supplied with the focus on integrating personal responses with critical, structured reflection. The marking criteria were no longer negotiable. From 1996 the journal's assessment weighting will be increased to 50% following enthusiatic approval from the external examiner.

Initially, students brainstormed criteria for assessment and came up with: Reflection, Honesty, Critical Awareness and Personal Input. In practice they found this too vague and felt that the journal was not an appropriate vehicle for summative assessment within such a loose framework and involving such personal material. In the second year the purpose of the journal was re-defined in a more academic way:

Your Learning Journal will be expected to:

- show the development of your learning across the course;

- illustrate a range of ideas;

- demonstrate a critical awareness of the central concepts on which the course focusses;

- demonstrate a structured response to course content;

- apply the concepts to the world/texts/practices that you know.

Evaluation

Early on there were strong student reactions to the use of the journal and even those who were committed to its use for personal reasons disagreed strongly with it being assessed. Nevertheless, by the end of the course the questionnaire feedback was mainly very positive. Students found the journal useful for learning through writing, for reflection on what was covered in class, and for the integration of personal experience and class-learning. Most students reported that it was useful to their learning in the light of the time it took. Students clearly valued the tutor feedback and found it helpful and gave them enthusiasm, confidence and confirmation of progress. Students continued to believe that it was too personal to be assessed. However, they also admitted that they would not have done it (and reaped the learning benefits) if it had not been assessed.

Discussion
This case illustrates the clash between formative and summative roles of assessment and the difference between personal diaries and more impersonal and analytical journals and logs. It highlights the need for clear guidelines and criteria and also the need to use evaluation feedback to modify and develop new methods.

Assessment of 'workbooks' on a Social Analysis course

Jessica Claridge, Staff Development Unit, University of Exeter

Innovator: Dr Grace Davie, Department of Sociology, University of Exeter

Course Context
Social Analysis is a compulsory course in year two of the BA in Sociology. The course was originally set up in order to:

- improve methods of training and to give students practical, 'in the field', experience;

- to make the course more relevant to the students;

- to make the work within the department more relevant to the local area.

Students undertake a social analysis project in groups of four which is assessed, individuals gaining the group mark which counts for 20% of their mark on the course. 30% of their marks comes from an individual 'workbook' which is a personal log of the work undertaken on the group project. This provides an individual mark to balance the effects of the group mark for the project. The other 50% of marks comes from an examination.

Workbooks are used:

- to produce a product in addition to the group report so as to provide a mark for each individual without additional tasks having to be set;

- to give the students training in using this classic sociological tool;

- as a way for the students to 'hold on to' the topic.

Information about the use of the workbooks is given in writing in the initial session at the beginning of term. Students are given clear instructions on writing the workbook in the briefing. They are also given sight of a good workbook from a previous year. Students are expected to keep this workbook throughout the project. Workbooks are used to record who the students saw, what they did, readings and sociological reflection. Although students may be reminded about keeping them, the workbooks are not taken in at all during the project and there is no formative feedback or mid-way discussion. It is regarded as the students' responsibility to maintain them. They are collected in for summative assessment before the final presentations take place.
Criteria are specified for marking:

1. Content: (a) substantive; (b) sociological

2. Organisation

3.   Completeness

4.   Authenticity – has the workbook been reconstructed? If it is obviously reconstructed, rather than having been written continuously, it is marked accordingly

5.   Literature review.

The values that inform criteria and judgment are considered to be: objectivity, imagination, reflection and sociological reflection, careful analysis, the capacity to remain detached, and the capability to be aware of theoretical implications.

The workbooks are marked according to normal conventions, i.e. by two internal markers, and moderated by an external examiner.

Evaluation

The course seems to work well. The practical methods of assessment of the project reflect one of the aims of the whole course which is to show that methodology is not a detached or separate activity but has to be part of substantive investigation involving a theoretical standpoint.

Though there are occasionally differences of opinion, as naturally occur when there are differing schools of thought on the way one might look at a topic, inter-marker reliability is high and there is a wide distribution of marks.

Bibliography

Hammond, M. and R. Collins, (1991), *Self-Directed Learning: Critical Practice*, London: Kogan Page

Hettich, P. (1990), 'Journal writing: old fare or nouvelle cuisine?', *Teaching of Psychology*, 17, pp. 36-9

Marshall, L. and R. Rowland, (1993), 'Keeping a personal journal/diary', in *A Guide to Learning Independently*, 2nd edn, Buckingham: Open University Press

Potts, D. (1981), One-to-one learning. In D. Boud, ed, *Developing Student Autonomy*, London: Kogan Page

Rainer, T. (1980), *The New Diary: How to use a journal*, London: Angus and Robertson

Selfe, C. L. and F. Arbabi, (1986), 'Writing to Learn: Engineering Students' Journals', in A. Young and T. Fulwiler, eds, *Writing Across the Disciplines: Research and Practice*, Upper Montclair: Boynton/Cook

Selfe, C. L., B. T. Petersen and C. L. Nahrgang, (1986), 'Journal Writing in Mathematics', in A.Young and T. Fulwiler, eds, *Writing Across the Disciplines: Research and Practice*, Upper Montclair: Boynton/Cook

Talbot, M. (1994), 'Learning Journals for Evaluation of Group-based Learning', in L. Thorley and R. Gregory, eds, *Using Group-based Learning in Higher Education*. London: Kogan Page

Walker, D. (1985), 'Writing and reflection', in D. Boud, R. Keogh and D.Walker, eds, *Reflection: turning experience into learning*, London: Kogan Page

Zubrick, A. (1985), Learning through writing; the use of reading logs', *Higher Education Research and Development Society of Australiasia News*, 7, 3, pp. 11-12

4 Using Projects

Introduction

Projects are now amongst the most common form of undergraduate coursework assignment as well as being used in the final year as major pieces of work as an alternative to dissertations. In postgraduate courses projects may constitute the only form of assessed work and may take up more student time than any other element of the course. They are used:

- to provide a vehicle through which students learn: researching a topic for themselves rather than being taught. Projects are often employed in order to provide a framework for extended periods of independent study with no specific educational objectives.

- to provide practice in the use of methodologies or forms of analysis, for example through case studies, experiments or short research studies;

- to relate academic forms of knowledge to complex real world problems;

- to develop professional skills in tackling real world problems;

- to set neutral or objective scholarly study in political or ethical contexts;

- to generate a major product such as a design;

- to link themes or topics dealt with separately within a taught course;

- to link disciplines or contrasting forms of analysis or discourse otherwise tackled in isolation within taught courses.

As with many other student centred methods there can be conflicts between the way a project would be run to maximise learning (an emphasis on process) and the way it needs to be managed in order to assess it properly (an emphasis on product). Resolving these conflicts is what makes project work successful.

Practical matters

Projects vary greatly in form along several dimensions the most important of which concerns who determines the choice of topic: the tutor, the student or some in-between mechanism involving constrained choice or negotiation. Other important dimensions include the source of learning materials (whether the tutor provides the key learning materials for the student, such as case studies, or the students find their own resources) and the degree of structure. Projects have many associated forms and names.

Thesis, dissertation, extended essay

Here students normally choose a topic, sometimes from a list provided by a supervisor, and research it largely independently, producing an extended written product. The product is characteristically marked by the supervisor and one other person after submission, with no intermediate stages or deadlines and with little imposed structure to the project.

Case study

Here students are provided with a range of relevant documents about the history of an incident (for example an accident or industrial relations disaster) or the development of a product, organisation or business, and are required to analyse the case, drawing conclusions or making recommendations about how the incident should have been handled or how the business should be developed in future. The case may involve a real situation (for example, studying an actual business rather than only documents about one) and documents or other information may be initially withheld until students realise what information they need and make specific requests. Large and complex case studies may be highly structured, with students being required to document each stage (such as 'identification of context', 'identification of problem', 'generation of alternative solutions', 'criteria for selecting solutions', 'selection of preferred solution', 'evaluation of selected solution', 'plan for implementing solution', 'plan for evaluating implementation'). Marks and criteria may be associated with each of these stages and students may be assessed largely on their ability to undertake these steps rigorously. Conclusions from the case study – the product – may be less important than the way the conclusions were reached.

Design project

Here the goal is the production of a visible product: a design or artifact. This product may be marked independently of the way it was produced. Fine Art is highly product-oriented, for example. However, where the process is important this too can be assessed, for example, through the use of portfolios or intermediate deadlines and submissions. Architecture students usually present portfolios containing early design studies, background research and so on, alongside their final models and drawings. Engineering students often have draft designs assessed and approved before they proceed to construction and testing.

Experiment or investigation

Here students are normally being inducted into the processes and techniques of scientific method within their discipline. Whether an experiment 'works' or a clear result is achieved may be less important than whether the literature has been adequately reviewed so that the study builds on existing knowledge, whether hypotheses have been formulated appropriately, whether the experiment has been designed in a way which enables the hypothesis to be tested, whether data has been collected, analysed and interpreted appropriately, and so on. Normally, a conventional experimental report will be used as the product which is assessed. However, formal means or reporting experimental work can easily be used to cover up the thinking and processes involved. There may be a need for additional assessment elements such as a viva or interactive presentation which are used to assess students' understanding of the decisions made about experimental design.

Discipline specific tasks

Many disciplines have their own unique form of task which is used to pull together students' knowledge and skills acquired throughout the course. In Geology it is usually a fieldwork mapping project, in Social Work it is often a social case report, in Town Planning it may be a judgment on a major planning application, in Computing the writing of a substantial computer programme, in Clinical Psychology a patient case study, and so on. In each of these subjects there is usually a distinctive form of product, the assessment of which involves professional as well as academic criteria which are quite different from those used to assess essays or conventional academic products.

Size of project

The Open University uses projects which vary in size from ten hours to 360 hours and project reports which vary in length from 1500 words to 12,000 words. Some of their courses involve a series of small, highly-structured and well-supported projects running alongside course materials while others involve a single independent project which constitutes the entire unit. While devices such as logs, portfolios and profiles are components of a larger scheme, projects are often the whole scheme and as a result they can be huge.

Supervision

Traditionally, project work has been closely supervised on a one-to-one basis with extensive, regular and expensive meetings. As student numbers have risen more cost-effective strategies have had to be adopted. These include:

- supervision via documentation: giving written advice and guidance, listing sources of information, assessment criteria and so on;

- scheduled supervision: where meetings are largely restricted to a limited number of fixed stages such as approval of topic, review of progress and review of first draft;

- pooled supervision: where students undertaking related projects are grouped and provide peer supervision in between group supervision meetings with the tutor;

- group projects where supervisors only meet groups working co-operatively on a shared project (see chapter 2, Assessing Group Work).

Key Issues

Why are projects being used?

It is easy to forget why project work is being used and to specify an inappropriate form of assessment product or assessment criteria. For example, professional forms of report writing look very different from academic forms and professionals use different criteria in judging them (for example brevity, clarity and practicality of conclusions). If a project is being used in part to bridge the gulf between students' academic studies and their subsequent professional role then these professional forms of writing and criteria should be adopted. If a project is being used largely as a way of capturing student interest and effort then requirements for a lengthy project report may be quite inappropriate and may distract students from their learning. The nature of the product and the criteria used to assess it should be selected to achieve the specified aims of the course and to generate appropriate learning behaviour, not simply to satisfy academic conventions.

Assessing products or processes

It is vital that project work clarifies the extent to which it is products or processes which are the aims and which will be assessed. The distinction between product and process assessment of project work is most stark in Fine Art. A painting or sculpture is usually expected to stand on its own with no commentary at all by the student who produced it. It could have been done in a rush with little effort and thought but still the product could be considered outstanding. Product is everything. In contrast, graphic art students often have to show portfolios of draft work showing how their designs have been arrived at and are expected to present and explain their designs. The quality of the product is moderated by evidence about process. Project reports in psychology are sometimes assessed almost entirely in terms of the quality of the way it was undertaken and whether an experiment 'worked' may be neither here nor there and process is considered more important than product.

What assessment criteria should be used?

Projects, because they are usually fairly large and contribute significantly to students' final degree results, are invariably double marked. But being in-depth work on a specific topic they are often outside the area of expertise of the second marker to a greater extent than for other double-marked work. It is common for first and second markers of projects to disagree widely in the marks they give because one is familiar both with the topic and the way the student worked on it while the other is familiar with neither. Second markers usually need special guidance concerning their role and the criteria they should be using. Sometimes second markers are brought in from outside specifically because they have the specialist expertise required. This is very common for architecture students' major studies, for example, and resembles the role of an external for a PhD. Here the problem is that the external was not involved in any negotiation of the brief or the purpose of the project and may bring criteria to bear which were considered irrelevant or even explicitly excluded from the project work. At Oxford Brookes University, Geography sends its external examiners all final year project proposals at the end of year two, and gains their approval and responds to their questions for clarification of the purpose, and criteria for assessing each project they will eventually double mark.

What feedback should be given?

The feedback it is possible to provide on projects can be amongst the most powerful and useful of all assessment feedback students receive, because students often commit so much effort to projects and care about the outcome. However, exam regulations often either forbid feedback or do not give it until the next course has started or even until after the student has left University. This is wasted learning opportunity. When projects operate over extended periods of time it is also appropriate to give intermediate feedback – explicitly and in writing – on plans and drafts. Some project assessment schemes even build in a proportion of the final marks for how well the student has responded to feedback in improving their project.

How big should the project be?

Projects are often defined, at least for formal examination regulation purposes, in terms of the number of words involved: for example, a 20,000 word project is common for final-year Honours degrees in place of a dissertation. Project work need not produce large products even when they involve extended periods of work, and are often better (for sanity of the student and the tutor) when they do not. They can be specified in terms of a collection of smaller pieces of work or even in terms of required contents of a portfolio (see chapter 9, Using Portfolios) which provides evidence of having tackled project tasks. However, in the absence of much class contact with which to calibrate the size of a project based course, it can be very difficult to judge the appropriate size of task or quantity of tasks students should be set. In the first case study below the external examiner recommended that the project have additional elements included to make it larger: while the quality of the work presented was commended, there was simply not enough of it.

Most courses have an associated number of total learning hours. For example a course involving a quarter of a semester is usually allocated 150 student learning hours and a final year project counting for 25% of final year marks would have 300 student learning hours. An attempt should be made to estimate how long the various components of projects should take students: this can help to judge what scale of project is realistic, help students to budget their time, and can also be a better guide than word counts. The aim should be to generate productive learning hours with as small a product as possible focussing on designing and planning the project tasks involved rather than on the product.

Does everything hang on the final report?

As projects can contribute 25% or even more to students' final degree results and can represent 100% of marks on a module, a great deal can hang on the final report. To reduce student stress and the chance of unexpected disasters it is often sensible for projects to include preparatory assignments, for example, involve a literature review, intermediate stages with partial reports and even draft final reports, all contributing to the overall mark. Staged work will make it more likely that students will keep up-to-date and take all the contributing sub-tasks seriously, and will also allow tutors to use assessment to re-orient students who are in difficulty or off target with their work. Many projects also include an oral presentation to the class, or a viva, as alternative ways to provide evidence of the quality of student work so that if the report is unrepresentative of the work which preceded it, students are not unfairly penalised.

How do students learn to undertake project work?

Students may need to work up to extended projects, tackling short and well defined projects using only a few simple skills at first and gradually increasing their size, duration, extent of choice and student decision-making involved and the level, sophistication and integration of skills involved. Students who have never undertaken a project before will struggle with a large open-ended project – a depressingly common experience of third-year students. Essay writing or lab report writing is a poor preparation for project work.

Apart from the academic research tools, equipment or subject knowledge involved, projects also involve generic study skills: literature searching, planning, extended writing, using features on a word processor such as footnoting and indexing, and so on. Students have been required to use these skills in earlier non-project activities (e.g. producing a literature review or annotated bibliography, designing studies and planning the stages of their implementation without actually carrying them out) in order to prepare them for project work. Ideally, project specifications should include lists of the skills required so that students can take steps to acquire the skills they lack. A proportion of assessment marks can be allocated to the use of these skills if it is necessary to get students to take them seriously.

Are criteria and marking schedules used and do they specify marks for different aspects of the project? What effect does this have on marks? – and on students?

It is vital that students understand what they are going to be assessed on: will it be use of techniques, awareness of the literature, justification of decisions, good results, scale of work, or what? Even when general criteria are stated in descriptive form students are usually given no guidance concerning the relative weights placed on criteria, and some, such as neatness, are likely to have completely different weights than others such as intellectual sophistication. It may be necessary to list criteria and allocate a maximum number of marks for each, revealing the weightings quite explicitly. It is also common for criteria to be mentioned in completely opaque ways, for example 'methodology'. Does this mean that if you have and state a methodology you will get all the marks?Are lecturers looking for strictly applied standard methodologies or do they have hidden values and are looking for features such as 'well justified imaginative departures from standard methodologies'. Some of the values of project work can be lost when criteria and marking schemes are drawn up. For example, values associated with creativity and risk taking may be overturned by concerns for methodological soundness or clear cut results. Unless the degree of novelty, creativity or risk is included explicitly in assessment criteria students will play safe – choosing well-established topics, questions and methodologies rather than really using the project as an opportunity to explore new issues in new ways.

It is relatively easy to use explicit criteria and marking schemes to orient students towards the kinds of learning activity, and the balance of activities, which are desired, and towards the production of appropriate forms of project outcome.

Do projects devour a disproportionate amount of student time for the marks they involve?

In practice, students often spend a disproportionate amount of time on project components of coursework and on project-based modules: up to three times as long as on conventional taught modules. At Oxford Brookes University it is common for students to 'clear the decks' of taught modules in the term they undertake their final year project and have as few competing demands as possible. Taught modules with project components characteristically capture more student time than do conventional modules. In terms of student learning on the project this may represent success. However, this may be at the expense of learning on other modules which are either less engaging or which make fewer demands. To determine the appropriate assessment weighting on project work it may be necessary to examine the proportion of student time it devours. While assessment weightings themselves influence the way students spend their time, projects appear to have an ability to grab time which goes well beyond what their assessment weighting would justify.

Do projects assess narrow parts of students' ability or knowledge?

Projects are sometimes introduced in order to pull together a wide range of knowledge and skills within a culminating task, but then students are allowed to specialise so that they only study a tiny area and use one method, perhaps one they have encountered before. It is often one of the few opportunities to go into depth on a topic of the students' own choice and this opportunity can be grasped with both hands. Project marks may be a very poor indicator of students' ability to undertake further research and may only indicate their knowledge of a narrow topic and the ability to use a single methodology, technique or piece of equipment. If breadth, flexibility and the ability to use a range of methodologies is required it will have to be designed into the project specification and into assessment criteria: for example, awarding marks for the use of diverse methodologies or the consideration of a range of cases or problems from diverse perspectives.

Is plagiarism an issue?

The often specialised foci of projects and the possibility of supervisors and markers not being personally familiar with the areas in which students are undertaking their project, offers students unparalleled opportunities for plagiarism. Access to electronic sources and word processing add to the problems and plagiarism can be very difficult to spot. The exchange of completed project reports between Universities and even between years is becoming more common. Safeguards include explicit guidelines and tutor briefings and explicit regulations with well understood penalties. But it may be necessary to introduce additional assessment elements, such as vivas or project exams, to test students' understanding of the content of their project reports, or rely more on evidence of work undertaken (such as through portfolios or logs) than on the product – process is harder to plagiarise!

Is the amount of supervision taken into account?

Supervisors vary enormously in the extent to which they generate ideas for projects, formulate and review detailed plans, provide detailed and regular support throughout and comment on final drafts. Some students will work almost entirely alone, managing all aspects of the project themselves while others are almost totally dependent on their tutors. Some tutors also feel that the quality of the product is a direct reflection on their competence or personal standing and go to extraordinary lengths to ensure that their students always produce very good work to the point where this is almost indistinguishable from the tutor's own work. If it is the product alone which is assessed then the extent of supervision will not be reflected in the mark. To take the extent of supervision and the extent to which students are responsible for the product into account requires an additional element in assessment. The supervisor can be asked to deduct marks from each section (initial plan, methodology, execution, final report, or whatever) where supervision materially improved the product. Alternatively, the supervisor can be asked to complete a proforma indicating the extent to which each aspect of the work was the students' own, for the guidance of the second marker who takes this information into account in their marking.

Is the size and difficulty of the task taken into account?

While essays of 1500 words or standard lab reports may not vary much in the amount of work they involve, projects can vary enormously even when a word limit is tightly specified. Some projects are simply much more difficult and more time consuming to undertake than others. It is common for some students to spend five times as long as others in the same class. Intellectual demands and sophistication may also vary greatly. It is possible to take these variables into account in allocating marks subjectively, or by explicitly rating the level of difficulty and size and then taking these ratings into account subjectively, or by using such ratings mechanically as a weighting on marks. For example a project rated as 50% larger than average could have a bonus of $50 \div 10 = 5\%$ of the mark added while another rated as 30% easier than average could have $30\% \div 10 = 3\%$ deducted from the mark. Second and external markers should certainly be made aware of the relative size and difficulty of each project if they do not have sufficient other experience or information to judge this for themselves.

Alternatively, individual project negotiations can be undertaken at an early stage to try to equalise the size and difficulty of projects undertaken (see also chapter 6, Using Learning Contracts and Negotiated Assignments).

Do projects produce the same range of marks as exams or conventional assignments?

Project work often produces higher marks than other types of coursework and much higher marks than unseen examinations: as much as three times as many projects gaining 1sts as other types of assignment. Students who struggle with other types of assessment can blossom with project work. The range of marks produced is often determined by the scope for students to specify their own projects and undertake idiosyncratic work. Tightly specified projects with clear steps and prescribed forms of outcome inevitably produce less diverse marks and, in particular, few outright failures. Open-ended work with plenty of scope for student decision making may produce some outstanding marks but also provides more scope for missing the target altogether and failing.

Each marker is likely to see fewer projects than they would normally mark essays or lab reports, perhaps only the six students they supervise instead of the sixty on a taught course. This means that there is less evidence about overall standards with which to compare an individual student's work and it is less easy to spread marks across a normal range. Adding the marks of a wide range of tutors all working largely in ignorance of overall standards can produce curious and unfair effects. This makes it all the more necessary to establish explicit criteria and standards and to employ double and external marking. However, external marking can be as random as first marking unless it is clearly guided.

Do markers agree?

The level of agreement between project markers and double or external markers is on a par with that of essay marking, in other words, pretty dreadful, but no worse than is normally considered acceptable. There is evidence that markers' personal preferences about methodology affects marks, with students whose approach matches the preferred approach of the tutor gaining much higher marks. Reliability can be improved by specifying criteria, by using marking schemes which allocate proportions of marks to components of projects or against specific criteria, and by training markers. As projects can contribute so significantly to students' final degree marks there is a particular need to address the issue of inter-marker reliability seriously.

Case Studies

Assessment of individual computer-based projects in Mediaeval Arts

Jessica Claridge, Staff Development Unit, University of Exeter

Innovator: Dr Avril Henry, School of English and American Studies, University of Exeter

Course Context

'Text with Computers' is a new full -time 80-hour 3rd-year project-based option course offered to any student within the School of English and American Studies. It is one of four courses students take in the year. Examination for each course is either by an 'option folder', which contains an average of four pieces of work, or by examination.There are similar 2nd year courses involving analysis of mediaeval texts without the use of computers.

Objectives

The project has explicit objectives:

• Literary objectives: to encourage detection, understanding and communication of literary structures by recording, exploring and conveying them in computer-graphic diagrams;

• Non-literary objectives: to encourage interdisciplinary skill-transference; to improve oral and written lucidity; to increase students' initiative and involvement; to encourage self appraisal.

The students can choose their own text to analyse but the analyses students undertake on texts are fixed: they have to discover and explain literary structures. Simple structures revealed by word-repetition are located on the computer. Students have to convey their findings not in an essay but visually, through diagrams created in computer graphics.

Students need to know how to use two pieces of software: NotaBene (word processing) and TextBase (text database) and to learn how to use two new pieces of software: CorelDraw (graphics) and PageMaker (desktop publishing). They evaluate literary criticism, study their text by diagramming and learn basic graphic design and typography.

Students learn the necessary project skills in 20 weekly three-hour practical sessions involving presentations of student work, guided practice and formative self-assessment. There is also written feedback from the tutor on an interim report. Students use a checklist each week to review their learning processes and progress.

Assessment

Assessment involves submission of a desk-top published booklet using 'PageMaker'. This involves an exercise in verbal, graphic and typographic communication, consisting of:

- cover design produced in CorelDraw;

- title page: title, name-logo, course, etc. in CorelDraw;

- diagrams in CorelDraw, of structures in their literary text;

- commentary on the diagrams, citing conventions and critical approaches to their text final;

- a report on the learning process involved;

- a bibliography.

The criteria for assessing the finished booklet are discussed at the outset. Booklets are double marked internally by the School and a member of staff from the University Computer Unit's Arts Faculty base who is involved with the course. They are then externally moderated.

Evaluation

The first operation of the course resulted in high marks ranging from 2:2s to 1sts. The work produced by the students at the end of this first course was very highly commended by the external examiner. However, there were modifications to the method of assessment recommended by the external examiner. It was suggested that future students should be given a viva in order to obtain aural comments on the diagrams and also undertake more work. In particular, it was suggested that there should be an assessed essay as well as the booklet.

Project work in English Language and Literature

Diana Eastcott, Learning Methods Unit, University of Central England

Innovator: Phil Smallwood, Head of School of English, University of Central England

Course Context

'Modern Critics' is a twelve-week option on BA English Language and Literature degree. 30 students take the option, a mixture of third-year full-time students and fourth- and fifth-year part-time students, including some mature students. The students had experienced a range of teaching, learning and assessment methods on earlier years of the degree and most were in their final year.

The students set the agenda for the Modern Critics option by acting as a team of writers who identify an audience for a volume (or volumes) on modern critics. They then design and write the publication. The main issue that is being addressed by the course and its assessment method is the lack of a genuine audience for student writing and the somewhat hypothetical nature of most assessment tasks. The students on this course address a real reading public and the product of their work is disseminated widely. Most of the students are already 'critics' and will have written substantial quantities of critical material since their school career. The course aims to build on this existing knowledge and competence.

The students have some control over the curriculum content of the course, and the process of the course and its assessment as they themselves model the nature of critical communication.

Objectives

The general aims of the degree as a whole are:

• to develop the students' ability to read, understand, analyse and critically evaluate texts;

• to develop the students' ability to communicate successfully especially in writing;

• for students to appreciate the relationship between their studies and contemporary social contexts;

• to enable the students to acquire skills which will equip them for their future careers.

Assessment

The objectives of the assessment task described in this case study are:

- to test the students' ability to work together towards a specific public or publishable outcome;

- to examine the students' critical awareness of the modern critical scene;

- to test the students' ability to contribute critically to thinking about modern critics.

It was clearly stated that assessment involved individual and joint work.

Students taking the course were given the task of designing and producing a public or publishable outcome on the topic of modern criticism. They had freedom over the choice of audience and once the decision on audience had been made certain decisions arose from this choice, e.g. scope, length and style of publication. The Course Tutor acted as editor and set deadlines to model the constraints of working within a 'real' publishing context. There were no excuses for missing deadlines!

After extended debate the agreed objective was to produce a learning pack to help teachers and students in Schools and Colleges to come to grips with aspects of the modern debate about criticism. The option group decided to divide into five separate sub groups. Each group concentrated on a different aspect of the theme, the purpose being to produce a distinctive but complementary contribution to the whole.

A feedback session was held half way through the course to check on progress. Students produced an individual interim report for this date (approx 1500 words) to include: indication of personal critical input to the work of the sub-group, reading in modern criticism, and feelings about the reading. The document was marked by the tutor as a progress report and marks counted towards the final assessment of the option.

Students were clearly advised by the tutor in writing of the final deadline for the whole learning package which was to be collected from all group members, compiled with written material in high quality typeface, and arranged ready for distribution.

The final mark for the learning package counted for one eighth of the overall Part Two mark for the degree.

Additional marks were available to all students for the success of the package as a whole. Thus, individual marks were awarded within a range according to the overall success of the product.

Individual marks were allocated according to the objectives, bearing in mind the approach to the chosen aspect of the topic and evidence of thought about its place in the whole publication. The marking was by the Course Tutor, followed by second and third marking and moderation by the External Examiner. The External Examiner did not alter any of the marks and commented very favourably on the standard of work.

The final products were a series of booklets and a video tape. The video included interviews with cinema audiences and 'A' level students.

Evaluation

The Course Tutor wrote a critical report on the option for the External Examiner in which he commented that the results were of a good standard. He also made several useful observations on the course in practice:

- the overall shape of the project which was organised as a group decision on thematic lines was difficult for some students to come to grips with. It demanded a broad level of awareness beyond individual work;

- some students are inspired by working with others to move towards video rather than written form. However, other students were initially inhibited by working in groups;

- there were considerable variations in the level of understanding of the task, between different groups and individuals within groups. Some found it hard to get beyond the form of the standard 'essay';

- some students ignored issues of standardised editorial/presentation style and had made contributions which were too long and did not fit with others from the sub group.

Students were asked to complete a brief questionnaire evaluating the course:

- the majority of the students responded that they found the experience of writing about criticism 'satisfyingly problematic';

- a small proportion of the students would have welcomed a more 'content based' approach to the topic of modern criticism;

- over half of the students enjoyed the experience of the course 'a lot,' the others enjoyed it 'on and off'.

Discussion

In this case study there is a real link between the assessment and the content and process of the course. The content of the course is determined by students' choice of critics and the audience to write for, and the tutor makes brief inputs on content or on the process of working towards a publication, at the relevant points. The whole shape and nature of the course is determined by the choices made regarding the assessment.

One of the aims of the degree is for the students 'to acquire skills which will equip them for future careers'. This course and its assessment are an exercise in practicality and realism in terms of negotiating with the tutor and other students.

As the topic for the course is modern critics, the students practise criticism in the process of the course as well as writing about it. For example, they make judgments about standards of quality, about what is and is not acceptable for the publication. The students also develop a critical sense in relation to each other, which can be confidence boosting. Students are encouraged to do their very best work.

In the future the Course Tutor planned to incorporate an event for an invited audience into the assessment.

Bibliography

Adderley, K., C. Aswin, P. Bradbury, J. Freeman, S. Goodlad, J. Greene, D. Jenkins, J. Rae and O. Uren, (1975), *Project Methods in Higher Education*, Guildford: Society for Research into Higher Education

Allison, J. and F. A. Benson, (1983), 'Undergraduate projects and their assessment', *Institute of Electrical Engineers Proceedings*, 130, A, 8, pp. 402-19

Cornwall, M. and D. Jaques, eds, (1977), *Project Orientation in Higher Education*, London: University Teaching Methods Unit

Edwards, D. (1982), 'Project marking: some problems and issues', *Teaching at a Distance*, 21, pp. 28-36

Harding, A. G. (1975), 'The objectives and structure of undergraduate projects', *British Journal of Educational Technology*, 4, 2, pp. 94–105

Henry, J. (1994), *Teaching Through Projects*, London: Kogan Page

Jaques, D. (1988), *Supervising Projects*, Oxford Polytechnic: Educational Methods Unit

Society for Research into Higher Education (1985), *Project Work in Higher Education*, Guildford: SRHE

5 Assessing Skills and Competencies

Introduction

Assessing skills, competencies, abilities and capabilities instead of only knowledge, is one of the major changes currently taking place in higher education and the professions. This is a change involving fundamental reconceptualisations of the purpose of higher education and the design of curricula. Here the focus is on assessment rather than on aims and at a stage in the development of methods at which most curricula have not yet changed radically even if assessment of skills has begun. The assessment of skills is undertaken in order:

- to acknowledge and give weight to skill components of existing courses and assignments, for example, the oral communication skills involved in a seminar presentation;

- to introduce new elements and emphases to otherwise content-dominated courses, adding components to curricula;

- to produce evidence for profiles or records of achievement which document individual students' capabilities rather than only a degree classification;

- to meet and fit in with external curriculum design frameworks, for example, in BTEC courses, or professional validation requirements, for example, in Law Society Legal Practice courses.

Practical matters

The role of assessment in skill acquisition

Skills are acquired through practice and feedback. Without feedback skills do not improve. Formative assessment is therefore more important, and needs to happen more frequently, than for other forms of learning. So central is this formative role that ability-based curricula often describe their approach as 'learning through assessment'. Asking students to tackle a single team task and assessing their team skills the first time they do this, without any prior practice or feedback on their skills, may be totally inappropriate. Summative judgments of final levels of achievement which produce marks may need to happen seldom and can operate in a different way than regular formative assessment.

Assessing skill components of existing assignments

The most common approach to assessing skills is to identify the skill components of existing assignments (such as use of evidence in support of arguments in essays or graphical communication of data in lab reports) and to give feedback or allocate marks explicitly in relation to the use of these skills. This may involve rating scales or headings for each sub-skill involved. Even simple forms listing skill components which are used to prompt and structure feedback, but which are unrelated to marks, can have a dramatic effect on students' focus of attention and hence their skill development, simply by highlighting the skills involved. The use of 'Assignments attachment forms' (see Brown et al, 1994) may be all that is necessary here.

Modifying assignments to involve skills

Assignments can be modified to increase the range or prominence of skills involved and make them more visible and easier to assess. For example a report can be required to be presented orally and visually to a static video camera to emphasise certain communication skills not evident in more leisurely seminar presentations, or reported in a 500-word magazine article and poster instead of in an essay. Annotated bibliographies can be added to assignments to develop and assess bibliographic skills, or seminar presenters required to take total responsibility for setting up and leading the session in order to assess group management skills. Reports can be required to be word-processed and include tables and graphs generated from a spreadsheet created from an electronic data base, to develop IT skills. In each case there would need to be a clear specification of the skills involved and the criteria used to assess them. There may also need to be advice or training in the use of the skill: presentations to a static video camera without prior training are invariably awful!

Designing assignments specifically to assess particular skills

Some skills, such as interviewing, managing finances or creative problem solving are simply never involved in conventional academic courses and the assignments they set. In recent years there has been an explosion in the diversity of tasks students have been set, partly in order to involve a wider range of skills and offer opportunities to assess these skills. Sometimes the projects tutors invent are so engaging they develop a life of their own and their purpose is forgotten, together with a realistic opportunity to assess the skills they were originally intended to involve. For example, teams of students are sometimes asked to mount conferences or other commercial events, partly in order to develop and assess financial skills. But the financial components of such projects may be very small, involve limited skills and be undertaken by only one member of each team. It might be much more efficient, and provide a much better basis for assessment of financial skills, to set paper and pencil assignments specifically concerned with financial skills to be tackled by each student independently.

Assessing many skills at once

It can be possible to use some learning processes to assess many skills. For example, a group project can be used to assess project management, creative problem solving, teamwork, leadership, written communication, and oral communication, all at once. In medicine projects and problem-based learning are being used to assess a whole range of competencies at once, using profiling methods. However, it is difficult to assess a wide range of skills properly and this often leads to superficial and unsatisfactory outcomes. It has been common in the early stages of the development of skill-based curricula to try to pack in as much as possible everywhere possible. More mature curricula adopt a targeted approach. For example, one module might target library and writing skills, the next written and oral communication skills, and the third team and project management skills. Pathways through degrees might involve a progression in the development and assessment of specific skills, with teamwork being assessed just once in eight modules in year 1, once in year 2 and once in year 3, the assessment concentrating on more advanced skills in each of the three modules. It is probably better to assess seldom and properly if marks are involved. Students can still be involved in team work in other modules in order to develop their skills, but their team work skills need not, and probably should not, be summatively assessed every time.

Profiling

Profiling (see also chapter 8, Using Profiles) often involves scanning across a range of student experiences and assessments, extracting their skill elements, and then attempting to document an overview of the skills developed. As a way of orienting students, encouraging reflection, and setting personal targets for developing further skills, this can work very well. Aided by a meeting with a skills tutor or, as in some institutions, the student's personal tutor, on a regular basis, this can be an excellent way of pulling together otherwise disparate learning experiences. As a way of assessing the level of skills acquired so as to provide worthwhile evidence to subsequent employers it leaves a lot to be desired. The fact that a tutor signs a profile cannot substitute for the rigorous assessment of skills through observing performance. Second-hand judgments based on a range of assessments undertaken by a range of others in different contexts, based on varied definitions of skills and involving varied criteria and standards, is unlikely to provide a sound basis for rigour and reliability. Even where profiling is comprehensive and compulsory institutions often nevertheless decline to validate the final profile because they simply cannot guarantee the standards involved in the same way they can with conventional assessment.

Training assessors

Assessors need to be inducted into assessing skills, becoming familiar with definitions of skills, with criteria and with standards, learning to make judgments from the new kinds of evidence they will be expected to assess (such as live performance rather than documents) and calibrating their judgments with their colleagues to produce a consistent approach. If those involved in marking can have some say in forming criteria and rating scales and the design of assignments, they are more likely to internalise the values involved and take a serious and consistent approach. Implementing externally designed and imposed frameworks is not a recipe for quality of judgment.

Training students as self and peer assessors

Because assessing skills is so time consuming and because the development of skills requires frequent practice accompanied by formative feedback, tutors can rarely cope with the volume of work involved. Almost all successful skill development programmes involve students in self and peer assessment. Students need to be able to judge their own level of skill and notice for themselves what they need to improve, and they need to calibrate their judgments against those of others, and use others' feedback to improve. Teaching students how to make judgments about skills, how to give feedback constructively, and how to take feedback is an important part of any skill assessment system. Initially, students will need clear observation and feedback forms and checklists and clear guidelines (see also chapter 7, Using Self and Peer Assessment).

Key Issues

Defining skills and their components

One of the main problems facing the assessment of skills is that few people seem sure about what, exactly, they are assessing. Institutions and Departments which adopt comprehensive approaches to skill development, often as a result of the Enterprise in Higher Education initiative, each have their own list of 'transferable' or 'enterprise' skills. These lists look tantalisingly similar and yet confusingly different. Different labels are used for similar skills (for example 'group work skills' and 'co-operative learning skills'), specific labels are categorised differently: for example, should 'time management' be categorised as a management, organisational or personal skill? Many skills appear to be omitted by oversight and there seems to be no rationale for some skills, such as those involved in interpersonal influence, negotiation or teaching, being present in some lists and absent from others.

Even when it comes to such universally included elements as 'oral communication skills' what this label is seen to include varies enormously. This is not just a consequence of context or curriculum differences. Even when you get down to specific instances where skills are demonstrated, such as in giving a seminar presentation, there is almost no agreement as to what the skill concerned actually consists of. Does the skill of giving a seminar presentation include use of audiovisual aids? And if so, what is it about their use which indicates skill? There is a tendency to try to address these questions by endless subdivisions and ever more detailed specification until skill lists take pages of fine print to list and are quite impossible to test simply because there are too many of them. A level of specificity is also reached where it is not at all clear that the skill is necessary or even likely to be effective in achieving desired ends. For example, I have seen seminar presentation skills broken down into components such as 'specification of the objectives of the seminar' but this is clearly not a necessary element of an affective seminar or ability of a skilful seminar presenter.

An alternative approach is to specify a small number of broad 'abilities' defined independently of their component skills. Alverno College's list is: 'Communication, Analysis, Problem Solving, Valuing in Decision Making, Social Interaction, Global Perspectives, Effective Citizenship and Aesthetic Response. Each of these abilities is thoroughly defined but not in a reductionist way.

Of course, defining what is being assessed is not exactly a strong point of conventional assessment, most markers relying on 'knowing what a B - grade essay is when I see one' rather than on any more explicit definition of quality.

Defining standards and progression

There is often a shared sense of what a 'degree level dissertation' looks like, even though this may be difficult to pin down and leads to variations in marks between markers. However, there is almost no shared sense of what 'degree level' group skills consist of or what the difference between first-year and third-year group skills should be. External examiners are as yet of little help in this because they have no idea either. There is also the problem that what represents 'degree level' IT skills for an English student may seem rather basic to an Engineering student, and what might seem 'degree level' written communication skills to an Engineer might seem illiterate to an English student. This is not a problem unique to skills, it affects levels of knowledge of such things as statistics and languages which are taught at very different levels in different subject areas. But it does mean that there have to be local rather than institutional definitions of standards.

If students are to progress in their skill development – and most curricula assume that there is progression – then there have to be definitions of levels of skills which can be used in assessment to track this progression. Such definitions are currently extremely rare. In modular courses where students study in several subject areas the differences in local definition and lack of clarity about levels could, in theory, cause students huge problems, though, in practice, standards for skills are generally too low to challenge students much.

Are skills discipline-specific?

In Law, interpersonal skills means interviewing and negotiation, written communication skills means drafting, and oral communication skills means advocacy. Most disciplines have their own versions of skills embedded in their values and professional practices. The use of these skills is also highly content and context specific. For example, it is not possible to show effective advocacy skills if you do not know the law and understand its application to the specific case involved. In such contexts it can be quite difficult to extract the element of skill from the overall effectiveness of a performance without robbing it of its validity. While skills can be taught and assessed separately it is only when the skills are integrated with knowledge that the competence of the student can be properly assessed. Whether it makes sense to allocate separate marks for 'use of skills' and 'knowledge' in such circumstances may depend more on the effect this has on students' priorities and learning behaviour than on the reliability or meaning of the marks produced.

Are skills integrated?

Some institutions teach and assess skills largely independently of course content and content-based assignments, or even in separate short courses or modules devoted exclusively to skills. One of the main problems facing transferable skills is how poorly they transfer. Assessment of skills out of the contexts in which they will be used may provide a very poor indication of how competent students are at using the skills in context. As disciplines vary so much in the form even core skills take, disembodied skills development and assessment may not be a very productive activity.

Does assessment indicate whether skills will transfer?

If evidence about students' level of skills is to be of value to employers it must indicate something about how skilful the students are likely to be in the employers' context. This means that forms of writing which are assessed should resemble the forms of writing used in employment: reports, bids, briefings and papers rather than essays. Forms of interpersonal communication should resemble committees or courts of enquiry rather than academic seminars, and so on. There is little point in going to a great deal of trouble assessing skills which bear little resemblance to those employers need. There is very little evidence in the UK that skill development in higher education actually makes any difference to students' employment and the predictive ability of assessment of skills has not yet been established.

What are the administrative implications of assessment of skills?

Because skills and competencies tend to be assessed separately and on several occasions, and because the development of skills is often tracked across modules or an entire degree rather than being completed within a single module, the administration and paperwork involved can easily mushroom. The way the assessment of NVQs has boosted the fortunes of filing cabinet manufacturers is legendary. Comprehensive skill assessment schemes require their own administrative systems and even computer-based systems to keep track of the information involved and normally require one person, perhaps a profiling tutor, to take responsibility for keeping track of each student.

Within individual modules it may simply mean a more complex reporting system with more separate items of information being collated, probably requiring the use of a spreadsheet, and more time-consuming external examination arrangements.

Are criteria for judging achievement of competencies clearly stated and understood by students?

I have seen Health Visitor students being assessed on their 'interpersonal skills' with no definition of what interpersonal skills means, no criteria and no standards, and with failure to demonstrate adequate interpersonal skills capable of preventing their further progress on the course. Not only could students not have explained what skills they were being asked to display but their tutors were not able to help them. If students are to develop their skills they need a clear sense of what they are aiming at: definitions, examples of skilful behaviour and examples of what they are not supposed to demonstrate. A label on a rating scale is not enough.

Are gradations of skills clearly described?

It is not sufficient to have clear criteria, there need to be standards as well and intermediate gradations between incompetence and total competence need to be clearly defined. It is not much help to a student being told they are rated three on a five point 'leadership skills' scale if the meaning of 'three' is unspecified. It is also, of course, impossible for tutors to assign such ratings with any reliability or meaning without each point on the scale being defined, probably in terms of observable behaviour. Alverno College have explicit public definitions of levels for each of the eight abilities their curriculum aims to develop and both students and tutors use these definitions, and 'models' of each level, to guide their judgments. It may not be appropriate for marks to be produced automatically by adding ratings, but neither should they be the result of global subjective judgments unconstrained by definitions of skills, criteria or standards.

What evidence about skills is available to be assessed?

It is common to assess teamwork without ever having seen a team in operation, using products of teamwork or self-reporting as the only evidence. Even where evidence from observation is available more emphasis is placed on products: for example, where a seminar paper is marked after a seminar presentation has been observed. The quality of products can give a very misleading impression of the quality of the processes through which they were produced, as any science tutor will confirm about lab reports which are often pure fiction. If skills are to be assessed properly then they must often be directly observed and assessed at the time. If second markers or external examiners are to be involved then sample video recordings should be made to, at the minimum, illustrate what a 'grade B' seminar presentation standard looks like or how a 'grade C' standard team functions.

With some skills the most important evidence comes from those directly involved in the 'performance' rather than from the tutor directly. For example, a tutor might find a presentation easy to understand but the student group to whom the presentation was addressed might have found it incomprehensible given their level of background knowledge. In counselling training, negotiation, interviewing or teamwork the views of other participants (the client, opponent, applicant or team member) is vital if a balanced judgment about the skill of the student is to be made. The complexity involved in this should not be underestimated. Assessing such skills properly is very difficult and time consuming.

Is what is assessed related to variable starting points or to absolute standards?

It is common for mature students and those with work experience to possess many 'core skills' to a much higher level than their 18-year-old fellow students. These differences may be much larger than those between levels of background knowledge or even levels of study skills. Does this prior learning mean that such students should be allowed to do well without learning much new? The assessment of skills provides more scope than usual for assessing progress made rather than standards reached. It also offers the possibility of students providing evidence that they already possess skills in order to exempt themselves from assignments and assessments. Assessing prior learning of skills can be as time consuming as assessing skills afresh and this route should not be adopted as an economy measure alone.

How are competent/not competent judgments made?

Some courses require not that a global mark is produced by aggregating scores obtained from the assessment of a range of individual skills, but that students achieve competence in each of a range of skills. Defining a threshold at which competence is reached and making a yes/no judgment is not logically harder than identifying a point on a rating scale, but the consequences of getting it wrong can be more serious. Where many skills are assessed at once, as is often the case in BTEC and NVQ assessments, these yes/no decisions can be made on extremely flimsy evidence and yet the sheer volume of assessment required makes more thorough assessment impossible.

How are pass/fail decisions made?

In competence based, yes/no, skills assessment it is usual for students to have to be competent in each of a range of skills before an overall pass/fail decision is made. Sometimes a mark is generated depending on how many skills the student is competent in. Sometimes the student can 'drop' a small number of skills from a long list, avoiding skills they are worst at even if they are skills they need. The rules governing how competence on individual skills translates into a course mark or pass/fail decision are often quite arbitrary.

How do students develop the skills?

It is becoming common for students to be assessed on skills they do not have and which they have been given no assistance to develop. Students are assessed on their teamwork without having been trained in teamwork skills and assessed on seminar presentations without having had any practice, advice or feedback, and so on. As a result the level of skill demonstrated is very low. Assessment standards are debased because a conventional spread of marks is allocated for a standard of skill which students already possessed before they started the course. This is like assessing students for their prior knowledge of topics not on the syllabus and not taught on the course. If students are to be assessed on skills there must be prior training in those skills.

How do tutors learn to assess the skills?

Assessing personal skills is not something most lecturers have done before: they often lack the skills themselves, lack the ability to recognise skilful behaviour and have no absolute sense of standards. In such circumstances their judgments are bound to be arbitrary, unreliable and unfair. Staff development and clear briefing is essential.

Is assessment reliable between judges and between different performances and different sources of evidence?

Markers have enough difficulty agreeing about grades for conventional content-dominated forms of assignment such as essays. The reliability of judgments of skills in the context of unfamiliar forms of performance must be expected to be low unless careful steps are taken such as specifying criteria and standards and undertaking marking exercises. Standards between markers and between different categories of students should be monitored closely. There is plenty of scope for personal bias, including sexism, racism and ethnocentrism. The Law Society is having a great deal of difficulty with the assessment of the legal skills of trainee barristers who are overseas students whose culture involves different social conventions to those in the UK and this is the subject of continued cases and reviews of practice.

There are also difficulties concerning variations in the context in which skills are demonstrated. It is normally assumed that one essay is much like another in terms of difficulty but student teams may pose very different levels of difficulty in terms of the group skills required to operate effectively. In legal skills training, negotiation skills are particularly difficult to assess consistently because of wide variations in the skill and approach of the person role playing the adversary: whether the person you are negotiating with is compliant or stubborn makes an enormous difference to how easy it is to negotiate.

Finally, it is usual for several different forms of evidence, from different assignments, to contribute to overall judgments about a specific skill. But would an essay, a magazine article, a poster and a seminar presentation all discriminate communication skills equally well? If they measure different things and some students are good at some of them and less good at others the end product will be that everyone will get very similar marks. If essay marks vary widely but the other three forms of evidence fail to discriminate much then it will be essay performance which ends up determining which students do well overall. There needs to be careful monitoring of which tests and which forms of evidence reliably differentiate the skilful from the unskilful.

How does marking relate to a normal distribution and conventional degree classifications?

It is common for mark distributions to be different for assessments of skill than for other more familiar components of assessment systems, with a high mean and a low standard deviation. Where marks are derived directly from adding rating scales the distributions obtained can be extreme. Until absolute standards have been established which would enable one to defend such distributions on the grounds that many students are actually outstandingly skilful, it might be safer to use a straightforward statistical transformation on raw scores to produce a mean and standard deviation identical to that of conventional assignments (for example a mean of 55 and a standard deviation of ten).

Case Studies

Peer assessment of interpersonal skills in Law

Jessica Claridge, Staff Development, University of Exeter

Innovator: Dr Jeff Smallcombe, Department of Law, University of Exeter

Course Context

The Law Department takes approximately 107 LLB students every year. It also has Combined Honours students taking Law and Society, and Chemistry and Law. In all there are 120 students in each year group.

The Law Department has for a number of years mounted a small scale programme of voluntary workshops for students. They are skill-based, practical sessions aimed at giving students practice in skills they can use as lawyers as well as in other areas of life. These sessions have involved interviewing and negotiating skills and industrial tribunal preparation, as well as the more traditional mooting skills. Teams have been entered for the National Client Counselling Competition and national and international mooting competitions where they have acquitted themselves well. The department felt that there was now a need to develop these techniques and spread their benefit more widely.

Skill Development Programme

This new programme of student centred skills training is for 1st and 2nd year Law students. Students are also involved in the organisation and judging of the exercise, which has developed from the industrial tribunals and negotiating skills workshop run by the member of staff.

The full programme was piloted at the end of the academic year 1993 and involved students who had participated in workshops throughout the year, who knew the ropes. The programme was in the form of a competition between eight teams (6–8 in a team) drawn from single and combined honours students from 1st, 2nd and 3rd years. The teams competed against each other in both interviewing and negotiating, on a 'knock-out' basis over a two to three day period.

The idea of running a programme for a complete year group was put forward to the Department by its Teaching Committee. As well as receiving the approval of the Department, the programme has been given financial 'pump-priming' support by the University Staff Development Unit.

The programme operates during the last six weeks of Trinity Term. It involves the compulsory participation of all 1st and 2nd year Single Honours students and Combined Honours students and the voluntary participation of

Interdisciplinary Single Honours and Combined Honours students. The project is in the form of a 'knock-out' competition involving 16 groups of 1st-years and 16 groups of 2nd years (6–8 in each group). Volunteer 3rd year students act as judges in combination with members of staff.

The programme is in three parts, with all teams from each year joining in the interviewing and negotiating exercises. This will be followed by the finals which will involve interviewing, negotiation and also mooting.

The interviewing exercise involves conducting a full formal interview with a slightly reluctant or 'confused' client (who is responding on the basis of a prepared and realistic scenario) and proffering appropriate advice. The client would normally be a student. The negotiating exercise involves two teams each being given information relating to one side of a real-life problem or dispute and representatives from each team negotiating their way, if possible, to a compromise of their respective objectives or of the dispute in question. The final or mooting exercise involves two teams presenting reasoned argument in an adversarial manner on different sides of a legal action. The teams have to confer, work out their approaches to the matter in hand and brief the members of the team who will actually be representing them in the competition.

The performance of the teams is assessed according to predetermined criteria by panels of judges drawn from 3rd year students and members of staff.

The programme lasts for three weeks. The first two stages each last for one week and are preceded by a lecture covering the objectives of interviewing or negotiations, the rules of the competition, hints on practical aspects of each area and consideration of practical examples of the problems/scenario. At the end of this period, the winning teams in each area from each year compete against each other in interviewing, negotiation and finally mooting. All teams which are knocked out will be encouraged to watch the rest of the competition in order to improve their own techniques.

Assessment

Interviewing skills workshops continue to be held through the Michaelmas Term and negotiating workshops through the Lent Term. As in previous years, these workshops will be for volunteers. In 1992 there were about 50 volunteers for each course of workshops. Students who were part of the successful National Client Counselling Competition last year are eager to help with coaching and to train teams for the next competition. These workshops are run fortnightly. There also continue to be Industrial Tribunal groups for those students taking Employment Law.

These sessions all enable students to develop their skills in a safe environment before the main programme in Trinity Term, which could command quite a large audience if the whole department is present. Students are encouraged to learn from their peers, from staff and by going to watch professionals working in court and on tribunals.

Those judging negotiating are asked to assume a norm to be about 66%. If a negotiation is not settled, they make an award for achievements obtained up to the point of break-off of negotiations. If one group appears to unreasonably frustrate the settlement they deduct up to 10% of that group's marks. They mark on the criteria of:

1. Attitude:
    confidence
    assumption of character
    ability to communicate
    approach to exercise

2. Contribution to negotiation:
    team work
    script accuracy
    ability to compromise when necessary

3. Control of situation:
    persuasiveness
    improvisation when necessary
    ability to close

4. Achievement of targets:
    identification of potential targets
    mark as an overview of achievement.

This total is then divided by the number in the group, to give each an individual score, as tasks may change within the group.

Evaluation

The students had all had experience of working with the lecturer in one of his practical workshops or group sessions, so they had no difficulty understanding what was being asked of them. The instructions for taking part in the pilot were very clearly laid down for the groups by the lecturer. Everyone took the whole exercise very seriously. Judges were well briefed and judgment seemed to be fair. They all felt that they knew what they were doing. No one felt that he or she had not been treated fairly or that there was anyone involved who had not 'played the game'. From the students' point of view, as well as the lecturer's, the pilot seemed to work well. They felt they had gained a great deal of practical experience and confidence.

Discussion

At present the work done in the Industrial Tribunal workshops and exercises conducted in Negotiation groups does not go forward as part of any summative assessment. The work done during the pilot practical exercise was peer assessed and the winners of the competition gained from prizes donated by a local firm of solicitors.

None of the work done in either workshops or the full Trinity Term programme, nor the assessments reached, form any part of summative assessment of students. This does not stop students wishing to be involved. They see the value of the practical skills they are developing. There could be, with future developments, a place for some formal assessment of the more practical aspects of law, which could count, in some way, towards a final degree classification. At the moment, students put the practical experience gained on their CVs and the report back is that prospective employers are impressed.

The lecturer sees great value in the use of students to coach others and hopes that this will grow with the development of the programme.

The assessment of personal development on part-time BA Business Studies Course

Diana Eastcott, Learning Methods Unit, University of Central England

Innovators: Harinder Bahra and Julie Hartley, Business Studies, University of Central England

Course Context

The BA Business Studies (part-time) course involves students attending two evenings a week for five years. There were 65 students in 1991/92. The innovation described in this case study is the Business Workshop which takes place over the whole of year 2 of the course. The majority of the students are well motivated adults with business experience. In common with many part-time students, they are under pressure to balance personal, work and academic commitments. A critical review of the course identified a number of key issues that were to influence the future design and development of the course:

- there were no mechanisms for integrating work-based learning and the experience that students bring with them to the course;

- the course was modularised, increasing the likelihood of compartmentalised learning and an instrumental approach to collecting units rather than an understanding of personal business contexts.

Innovations on this course need to be seen in the context of increasing student numbers and the internal restructuring and modularisation of the Business School undergraduate courses.

The Business Workshop was introduced for the first time in 1990/91. It is designed to help students integrate their studies with their work experience and their personal and career goals. It is a self development exercise which encourages students to reflect on their past experiences and use the insights gained to plan for the future. The objectives of the workshop activities are:

- to raise students' self-awareness concerning their career and life goals;

- to provide an opportunity to relate theory to business practice;

- to help individuals to identify their personal learning needs, business skills and knowledge requirements;

- to enhance individuals' life choices and potential employability during and at the end of the course;

- to provide an opportunity to consolidate individual learning;

- to help individuals develop their problem-solving and decision-making skills.

The self-development activities are split into four sections:

- where are you now? – a reflection on past experience and present skills;

- where do you want to go? – an analysis of future aspirations and objectives;

- how can you achieve your goals? – the development of action plans;

- assessment.

Students are provided with a 40-page manual containing an outline of the workshop, instructions for 11 exercises and details of the assessment process. The workshop is introduced during a two-day residential meeting at the start of the first term, from then on the emphasis is on student centred learning. Students work through the exercises in the manual and are encouraged to be open about their findings, feelings and emotions. In addition, students are allocated a workshop tutor who runs 'clinic' based sessions where students can obtain advice and guidance at pre-booked times.

Assessment

The methods of assessment and criteria for assessment are set out for the students as part of the workshop manual. The assessment is the equivalent of any other unit on the degree and involves four elements:

		Types of Assessment	Length	% of marks
1.	Position audit	Report	1500 words	25
2.	Future-goals and objectives	Report	1500 words	25
3.	Action planning	Report	2000 words	25
4.	Presentation to peer group	Presentation	10–15 min	25

In order to pass the Business Workshop a student needs to achieve an average of 40% in total. Assessment components 1–3 are assessed by tutors and 4 is assessed by peers. Marks are moderated between the three tutors involved.

Presentation Assessment

Name..

Assessors...

Task...

COMMENTS   MARK

PRESENTATION:
Imagination
Atmosphere
Attractiveness
Impact
Use of visual aids

STRUCTURE:
Introduction
Objectives set
Well structured
Balance of argument
Conclusion
Objectives met

UNDERSTANDABILITY:
Content
Coherent/logical
Clarity
Uncomplicated

TIMING:
Under/over time (penalised)
Balance of presentation
Opportunities for questions

GUT REACTION (intuitive response):
Enjoyable
Interesting
Poor
I liked it
I didn't like it

The assessment concentrates on the quality of analysis and reflection on experiences by the students. It does not attempt to ascribe value to the actual achievements or successes of the students, but rather the way in which the students analyse the experiences and demonstrate their learning from them. The assessment process acknowledges that we have different views of achievement and success. A high mark would not necessarily be given to a student who had obtained promotion at work, but a good mark may be awarded on the basis of the person's analysis and reflection on this process. Students are asked to view assessment in the context of being a natural part of the learning process so that as well as contributing to grading it provides feedback for students and course teams. The criteria for assessment of the presentation are included in the form used to give feedback (see previous page).

The report required for Assessment 2 involves the following briefing:

Consider the information generated by the above exercises. (Life Line; Work Preferences; Value; Style and attitudes; Most and least rewarding job/roles; Your ideal next job/role). Produce a report reflecting on your personal objectives and your career/work objectives, including contingency plans, using the following headings: Short-term objectives, Medium-term objectives, Long term objectives.

Evaluation

Student reactions to the Business Workshop activities have been extremely positive. Many students admitted to finding it hard to reflect on what were sometimes personal and painful experiences. Some students felt that the workshop was the crucial element of the Course.

'It made you ask 'What am I? What do I want?' I began to see where I wanted to go, to explore opportunities, and I realised I could change and that it was up to me to realise my own potential.'

Material from the students' written reports indicated that the students took the exercises and assessment very seriously and many showed evidence of a high level of reflection and analysis. For example:

'By virtue of my race and class I was not totally accepted at school. This resulted in personal problems of a motivational nature. Later I was to realise that allowing others to influence my perceptions was to deny my self belief. Having realised this I have endeavoured to dismiss the perceptions of others and to strive to accomplish all that I truly believe I can accomplish.'

The tutors saw their role as that of a facilitator to help the students in the process of developing insights. Some students changed their jobs following the reflective work in the Business Workshop!

Discussion

Assessment of personal development is notoriously problematic. Is the person herself/himself being assessed, or their writing and presentation of themselves? There is often a very fine line here. Assessment of personal success is inevitably value laden, and criteria for success vary between individuals. By means of the strategy of concentrating on the analysis of experiences and the quality of learning as opposed to a basic description of the experience which an individual has had, the assessment on the Business Workshop deals effectively with some of the problems surrounding assessment of personal development. The key is for the students to demonstrate not simply that they had an experience, but what they have learnt from it.

Bibliography

CNAA/BTEC (1990), *The Assessment of Management Competencies: Guidelines*, London: CNAA Publications

Economides, K. and J. Smallcombe, (1992), *Preparatory Skills Training for Trainee Solicitors*, Law Society Research Study No. 7

Erwin, D. T. (1991), *Assessing student learning and development*, San Francisco: Jossey Bass

Felletti, G. and G. Colditz, (1979), 'An Educational Model for Assessment of Student Competence in Medicine', *Assessment in Higher Education* 5, 3, pp. 279-93

Gibbs, G., D. Jaques, A. Jenkins and C. Rust, (1994), *Developing Students Transferable Skills*, Oxford: Oxford Centre for Staff Development

Hughes, I. and B. Large, (1993), 'Assessment of students' oral communication skills by staff and peer groups', *The New Academic*, 2, 3. pp. 10-12

Jenkins, A. and L. Walker, eds, (1994), *Developing Student Capability through Modular Courses*, London: Kogan Page

Klemp, G. O. Jnr. (1979), Defining, measuring and integrating competence, *New Directions for Experiential Learning*, San Fransisco: Jossey-Bass

Loaker, G. and P. Jensen, (1988), 'The power of performance in developing problem solving and self-assessment abilities', *Assessment and Evaluation in Higher Education*, 13, pp. 128-50

Otter, S. (1992), *Learning outcomes in Higher Education*, London: Unit for the Development of Access and Continuing Education/Further Education Unit

Schulte, J. and G. Loaker, (1994), Assessing general educational outcomes for the individual student: Performance assessment as learning: Part 1. *Designing and implementing performance assessment instruments*, Milwaukee: Alverno College Institute

Usherwood, T. and D. Hannay, (1992), 'Profile-based assessment of student project reports', *Medical Teacher*, 14, pp. 189-96

Winter, R. (1992), 'The assessment programme – competence-based education at professional/honours level', *Competence and Assessment*, 20, pp. 14-18

6 Using Learning Contracts & Negotiated Assignments

Introduction

Learning contracts involve various kinds of explicit agreement, usually between an individual student and a tutor, about what learning tasks are to be undertaken, what the outcomes will be, (both in terms of learning outcomes and products which can be assessed), and how those outcomes will be assessed. In principle these agreements take the form: "If I agree to do this for this purpose and produce this kind of product to this standard, then I deserve to pass (or to get the following grade)". Learning contracts allow for considerable freedom and self-direction in learning while providing a framework which can be rigorous and meeting formal assessment requirements. Learning contracts take various forms:

- agreements about projects as a framework for supervision and assessment;

- agreements about work experience as a framework for work-based supervision and subsequent assessment;

- agreements about what modules and other fixed learning components will be undertaken in order to fulfil formal course requirements;

- agreements about independent study for a module or to fulfil the requirements of an entire Diploma or Degree;

- agreements about modest and bounded tasks such as essay questions, practical experiments or field work;

- agreements about how fixed objectives (e.g. involving competencies) will be achieved and demonstrated;

- agreements between members of project groups about the relative contributions of group members;

- agreements which include what the tutor will do in terms of supervision, provision of resources and feedback, to support the student in completing the contract.

Practical matters

Briefing

Many students are so used to teachers making all the decisions about what is to be learnt, and how, that the introduction of learning contracts often has to be undertaken with care and patience. Dependent students can initially feel frustrated, anxious and confused by the lack of structure and tutor guidance and may develop unimaginative contracts in a mistaken attempt to meet what are assumed to be the tutor's goals instead of developing personal goals which they care about. The purpose and potential benefits of contracts will need to be thoroughly explained.

Identification of learning needs

Many forms of learning contracts give students the freedom to specify their own learning goals and when this is the case it is often sensible if these goals are based on a thorough analysis of learning needs rather than on whim or fancy. In some contexts this may involve profiling of competencies or analysis of the demands of a job or career in relation to current competencies and knowledge. Not all forms of contract give students freedom to specify their own goals.

Preliminary research

It is often necessary for students to undertake some preliminary research into a topic before it is possible to formulate a sensible contract: to find out what is known, what is possible, what is interesting and what seems worth trying to achieve. For substantial contracts (e.g. for an entire qualification) this preliminary research leading up to the formation of the contract may last for 25% of the available study time. At Vermont College students spend four months developing a 'study plan' for the next 18 months of study and at the School for Independent Study at the Polytechnic of East London students used to spend two to three terms developing a learning contract for the next two years' work. If a group of students are formulating contracts in the same area it may be appropriate to offer teaching to make this research focussed and efficient. In some cases this research may involve a modest trial run at a learning contract in order to explore its implications and to develop negotiation and trust between student and tutor.

Preliminary negotiation and developing a contract

It is common for students to be asked to draw up a draft contract to discuss with a tutor or supervisor and for this to lead to more focussed research and needs analysis before a final contract is drawn up. For a substantial contract, as for a PhD proposal for example, this may involve several cycles of revision and tuning up. As this stage can be time consuming for tutors it may be possible for students to act as peer advisors, using a checklist of questions such as: What do you really need or want to learn? What would be the best way of learning that? What resources would you need for that? How long would that take? How would you know when you had done that well enough? The tutor is then left with the less demanding task of checking and final negotiation.

The written format of the contract

Most courses using contracts have a pro-forma with headings such as that in the Publishing course case study below. The most common headings concern learning aims, learning activities, resources which will be used (including people), learning outcomes, especially those which can be seen and assessed, and form assessment. Assessment may involve negotiated criteria but may also specify proportions of marks associated with elements of the outcomes (for example 25% for a literature review, 50% for a report and 25% for a portfolio of newspaper articles with annotations, if these were the three negotiated learning tasks).

Final negotiation

The whole point of contracts is that there is a balance of power between the student and the tutor instead of the assessment being controlled entirely by the tutor. However not everything need be negotiated and the power may be unevenly distributed. Each element of a contract may be determined by the tutor, negotiated, or determined by the student and either the tutor or the student may have powers of veto. For example the goals may be set by the course in the form of a set of competencies the student must exhibit. What may be negotiable may be the kinds of evidence the student may submit to demonstrate these competencies. The criteria may be fixed and assessment of whether the evidence the student eventually submits meets the criteria may be negotiated, but with a right of final decision by the tutor. In another context everything may be negotiable with no right of veto on either side but with an external examiner to control standards, independently of both tutor and student, who will use a set of fixed, if rather general, criteria. It should be stated clearly what is negotiable and what is not and who has the power.

In contexts where a range of competencies have to be acquired students may be permitted to formulate a series of separate contracts which, between them, meet the requirements: for example a contract concerning a budget report to demonstrate financial competencies and writing skills, a contract involving the production of a video of some interviewing to demonstrate interpersonal skills and a contract for an essay to meet requirements to demonstrate knowledge in certain areas.

Negotiating changes

It is common for students to feel the need to renegotiate the contract after a little while. Interests may change, pragmatic problems may make the achievement of the original goals impossible or standards may have been set unrealistically high. The right to renegotiate or a deadline beyond which further renegotiation is not permitted may be built in to the original contract or be a specified component of the course. There need to be ground rules about what can be renegotiated and what cannot and who has the final say, just as with the original contract.

Monitoring

Students undertaking contracts for the first time or undertaking substantial contracts are likely to need monitoring at one or more points along the way, just as with substantial projects. Monitoring can focus on which negotiated learning tasks have been undertaken, which skills and resources have been used and what further planning is necessary to complete the agreed contract by the agreed time to the agreed standard.

Outcomes

It is common for the outcomes of learning contracts to be much more varied than the outcomes of conventional study: for example video-tapes, testimonials, notes from research and so on instead of essays. Some of these products will not have well established academic expectations regarding appropriate standards and it may be very difficult to devise appropriate criteria and standards for every product in an equitable way. It is therefore common to specify an 'equivalence' to a known outcome such as "an outcome equivalent to a 5,000 word essay". Once such standards have been set it is very tempting for students and tutors to then use a 5,000 word essay for ease of assessment rather than outcomes more appropriate to the individual goals and learning activities involved.

Self and peer assessment

Given the degree of open-endedness already built in to learning contracts it is often sensible to maintain the involvement of tutors who have a sense of equivalence of standards across different contracts rather than involve self or peer assessment to directly determine marks or pass/fail decisions. Formative self-assessment is vital prior to negotiated assessment with a tutor and formative peer assessment can be a valuable input to self assessment.

Pass/fail decisions and marks

Contracts are best used in pass/fail situations where the decision rests on whether the outcome meets negotiated requirements or not. In some contexts students are allowed to negotiate a contract for a particular grade ("this is what I would have to do to get a 'B' grade") but the finer the discrimination required at the time of assessment the finer the judgment needs to be about the contract at the point of initial negotiation and specification of criteria. Marking the outcomes of contracts with a percentage poses all sorts of difficulties similar to those involved with marking projects of different levels of difficulty and different levels of student independence from tutors.

Involvement of externals

The final grade or mark is determined to a considerable extent by the way the contract is initially negotiated – especially what is negotiated about the nature of the final product and the criteria which will be used to assess it. In a sense the standard involved is largely fixed at the outset rather than being largely determined at the time of final assessment. For this reason if external examiners are to be involved they may have to approve the initial contract as well as being involved in seeing the final product. The student and tutor may need to summarise their assessment negotiation in order to explain the basis of their decision which the external examiner has to moderate.

Key Issues

Are objectives fixed or constrained in advance?

Fixed goals need not prevent the use of contracts. It is common on Certificate in Management courses operating under the Management Charter Initiative, which has specified competencies, to allow negotiation of the form of evidence students will present to demonstrate their achievement of each competence but there is no negotiation of objectives whatsoever.

What is negotiable?

As explained above it needs to be absolutely clear what is negotiable and what is not, including any deadlines or scope for renegotiation and especially how assessment will be undertaken.

What is the negotiation process, who is involved and who has power?

The negotiation process is often not specified but in the absence of any ground rules tends to take the form of the student making a fairly complete proposal and the tutor responding, within a single meeting. Alternatives can involve the tutor making counter proposals, the student's proposal being considered acceptable unless the tutor has prima facie evidence that it could not meet formal requirements or three way negotiation involving a work-based supervisor at a stage after the student and tutor have agreed a draft contract. The potential for student commitment to learning which comes from pursuing personally relevant goals always has to be weighed against the maintenance of common standards and the achievement of course goals and it is sensible to think through which of these should have most priority and so where the balance of power should lie.

How do students learn to set goals and negotiate?

Students may need to be taught how to set learning goals, indeed what learning goals are, and how to conduct a negotiation in an assertive, effective and non-confrontational manner. Tutors' greater negotiating skills may in themselves shift the balance of power. It is very helpful for students to see sample contracts and even to role play a negotiation prior to meeting a tutor so as to anticipate the tutor's perspective.

How do tutors learn to negotiate?

As learning contracts involve relinquishing at least some tutor power the form of negotiation which is appropriate is not one designed to 'win' an argument but one designed to foster the formulation of the most appropriate contract for the student within course requirements. Tutors not used to this kind of role may need a staff development event in which they experience contracting from both the tutor and student perspective in order to develop suitable approaches. When work-based supervisors are involved in three way negotiation of work based learning contracts they too will need briefing or training.

How is monitoring undertaken?

With the kind of open-ended framework contracts can provide students may have more rather than less need for supervision or at least monitoring, tracking student progress towards the achievement of what has been agreed.

What counts as evidence and how is it validated?

Contracts leave open the possibility of students providing all kinds of evidence that learning goals have been achieved. For example a student might propose that evidence of interviewing skills be provided in the form of a testimonial from a former employer. Would such evidence be allowed to count and how would its validity be established? Sometimes the negotiation of corroborating evidence can be enormously time consuming.

Whose criteria are used?

The first time students encounter contracts it is often helpful to limit the number of elements being negotiated and it can be particularly helpful for students to have a yardstick against which to calibrate the scale and standard of learning outcomes and products. When criteria are negotiated as well as products this may lead to a better match of criteria to idiosyncratic products but at the expense of comparability. It is useful for students to think through what would make their proposed products acceptably good enough but it may not be necessary to allow them to specify their own criteria to do this. It may be sufficient, for example, to provide a list of five criteria and then ask the students to propose how they would meet three of them.

How can levels and standards be determined? Are outcomes measured against (absolute) fixed standards or against (relative) negotiated targets? How do staff learn to judge products of unpredictable nature and quality?

It is difficult enough marking very different projects alongside each other to fixed criteria. Marking varied contracts involving all kinds of components to different criteria and standards will almost inevitably produce inconsistency, especially between markers and almost inevitably between double markers where the second marker has not been involved in negotiations. Where highly open-ended contracts are used there is a pressing need for tutors to discuss contracts and criteria with each other and to undertake comparisons of the size, difficulty and standard of both contracts and products in order to calibrate judgments. As it is common for students to produce very good work as a result of the commitment which accompanies learning contracts the issue of standards may not seem pressing. However there are always some students who do not complete contracts as agreed and it can be very difficult to decide what to do about this.

How are disputes handled?

In such an open-ended context it is inevitable that there will be disputes: about contracts which are vetoed by tutors as inappropriate or of too trivial (or ambitious) a nature, about criteria which appear to a student to be different from those involved in another student's contract, about a refusal to allow comprehensive renegotiation when a student changes their mind, about interpretation of the contract or application of criteria at assessment, or simple disagreement about whether a contract has been fulfilled or not. In such circumstances there needs to be a well understood system of adjudication. This might involve either student or tutor having the right to bring in an independent contracts 'ombudsman' whose decision is final.

Case Studies

Assessing Independent Study modules in Publishing

Chris Rust, Educational Methods Unit, Oxford Brookes University

Innovators: Ray Clench and Rosemary Roberts, Publishing, Oxford Brookes University

Course Context
'Independent Study' modules are one-term modules available as an option for any second- or third-year student. Different subject areas offer their own versions of independent study. Most involve negotiated project work of one kind or another though some involve work placements: for example, Education's independent study module is an internship. This case study considers how the 'Independent Study' module operates in Publishing, a subject area which provides up to a half of a modular degree within the large modular programme at Oxford Brookes University.

Assessment
The assessment method for Independent Study modules is unspecified and open to negotiation, as is the subject chosen by the student, within the following requirements:

•   it must be established in advance, as part of the approved module specification;

•   it must be agreed by the subject area concerned to be commensurate with the requirements of other single advanced modules offered by the subject;

•   it must be completed by students by Week 9 of the term in which the module is undertaken;

•   accompanying the final submission should be brief statements, set out on an appropriate form (see Appendix A) summarising the work undertaken, the time involved and how it has been spent, the facilities used, and the aim of the work.

It is the responsibility of the student to investigate and propose their choice of topic (although the module leader is obviously willing and able to help), and then choose an appropriate member of staff to act as their module supervisor. The student then negotiates the exact nature of their project, and the assessment criteria, with that module supervisor and completes an enrolment form. The proportion of marks allocated to each component of the learning tasks is also negotiated at this stage. There are no fixed criteria because the contacts vary so much in their content.

The types of individual study module undertaken tend to fall into one of the following five categories:

1. To develop further an area of interest derived from other modules, e.g. children's fiction is alluded to in a number of modules but has no module of its own, and is not specifically covered in any depth so it might be the focus for an independent study module.

2. Work experience in a related area. This is recommended to publishing students, but not compulsory, and if done is undertaken during vacations. Those students who wish can build an Independent Study module out of this experience by applying a critical analysis to some aspect of the company and its operations.

3. Research for a company. Sometimes stemming from work experience, and sometimes coming through a tutor, the student may undertake some research for a company and turn that into an Independent Study module.

4. Group taught course. If a module is withdrawn because there are insufficient students opting for it, but there is a group of students very interested in the topic (e.g. Analytical Bibliography) it can be done as an independent study module. This would comprise some linked seminars and group tutorials, rather than the full taught course, and much greater emphasis therefore on independent learning.

5. Illustrated Book project. This is rather different to the other four categories in that there is a prerequisite module (Typographical design and planning) and there are a definite set of requirements and assessment procedures. The purpose is for the student to see a book through every stage of production from conception to publication. They have to get, or write, an original text, find illustrations, design, set and print the book. Throughout this they have to maintain a work schedule and finally write a report. The assessment is divided 70% for the product, including the process of production, based on the work schedule, and 30% for the report.

All the Independent Study modules are marked by both the supervisor and a second marker, who is agreed upon when the project is near completion. On the rare occasions when these two cannot agree, a third marker is called in to moderate.

Evaluation

No formal evaluation specifically of the individual study module has been undertaken, but there is a general belief in both the School and the University at large that it is a valuable option. 'Independent study . . . clearly works as we have established it, and is appreciated by a significant minority of staff and students' (David Watson, Dean of the Modular Course, 1988). In fact the school included it in its original CNAA submission in 1982, and argues that it widens the opportunity to meet students' interests, and for study which would not be economically viable as a taught module. It allows for more vocational experience and also for the development of more specialist programmes of study. In addition, there are the general arguments associated with the benefits of self-direction and independent learning.

The Independent Study module option certainly appears to be steadily growing in popularity with the students. In 1991/92 a third of all final year students elected to do one.

Discussion

While theoretically the assessment is not prescribed, in reality all independent study modules have included a report of between 2500 and 5000 words, so in practice there are clearly limits to the scope for negotiation. While similar to a project or dissertation module at Oxford Brookes, Independent Study modules have some significant differences. The Independent Study module can theoretically be done any time in the second or third years, although in practice it is almost always done in the final year. The module is not as big as a dissertation in terms of what is expected, and there are less restrictions in terms of what form it may take and how it may be assessed.

At present students are limited to only one Independent Study module and there have been a number of Publishing students who would have liked to do both the Book project and one of their own but have been prevented by this regulation. However, the Field is currently under review, and the possibility of allowing the choice of up to two independent modules (providing they are significantly different) will be discussed.

Appendix A

OXFORD POLYTECHNIC

SCHOOL OF VISUAL ARTS, MUSIC & PUBLISHING

MODULE 5288 INDEPENDENT STUDY MODULE

SUBMISSION DOCUMENT

Please complete this form and attach it to your 5288 submission. This information will help future administration of the module.

Student Name...

Title of Module Submission..

....

1 From where did your idea for your independent study originate?

2 Did the work you undertook in the course of the module vary from that stated in Section C of your 'specification for independent study' (form M88)? Please detail.

3 In practice, how much time did the module demand, and how was it apportioned?

4 What facilities were used in the course of the module?

5 Was any other support that you expected lacking or deficient in any way, e.g. library, computer, technical, etc?

6 How many times did you meet for a tutorial with your supervisor? (Please tick)

   (a) once/twice   (b) three times   (c) four times   (d) five +

7 From the standpoint of the completed module, were its aims achieved? If not, please detail.

8 In retrospect, what principal gain did you derive from doing this independent study?

The use of learning contracts in an open learning module in Engineering

Jessica Claridge, Staff Development Unit, University of Exeter

Innovator: Dr David Buckingham, School of Engineering, University of Exeter

Course Context

The module described here takes place in term 3 of year 2 of a three year (BSc) or four year (BEng) Engineering course and is taken by 100 students per year. The degree programme has to be accepted by the accredited Engineering Institutions and there are constraints on the syllabus. The promptings for the course came from the need for training Engineering students in organisation and communication skills.

The rest of the degree programme could be considered conventional, both in terms of its teaching methods and its assessment. There had been, for some years, a communications course run in the first year and a good deal of individual and group project work later on in both the three and four year programmes, which was another impetus to set up the module.

Assessment

The 'Open Module' involves a negotiated project which is assessed.

1. Students are informed about the Open Module by letter at the end of the first year. This explains the nature of the module, the method of assessment and asks them to consider ideas of work they might like to do during the module. They have six months to think about it.

2. Midway through Michaelmas Term (two months before they start the module) they receive a pro-forma through the internal post with a deadline for return, on which they have to say what they would like to do. The co-ordinators look through the returns, discuss them and return comments to the students in writing towards the end of the Michaelmas Term. Students will either be told 'yes, go ahead' or 'no'. If it is 'no', then a meeting is set up to discuss concerns staff might have.

3. Final decisions are confirmed in writing, with copies to students' personal tutors and any advisers who may be identified. There is always an adviser. For general concerns it will be one of the co-ordinators, for technical matters specialist advisers are arranged by the co-ordinators. This is where a contract can be said to have been arranged.

Negotiation of the task and its learning criteria is frequently devolved to the specialist adviser. The co-ordinators keep an overview of what is happening.

4.   At the beginning of the Lent Term there is one meeting of the whole class with the co-ordinators to explain fully what they are looking for from the Open Module and to issue paperwork for the term. Every student receives a set of checklists (schedules) for the term. Each of these has the student's personal number on. These checklists are to enable the students to monitor and develop their ideas throughout the term and have to be handed-in each week to a definite deadline. If the deadline is missed, one grade point is lost from the final assessment.

The checklists change and develop through the term as the student develops. In this way students can monitor their own progress, shift targets and modify or expand their own aims as they go through the term. During the module, co-ordinators are available four afternoons a week on a surgery basis.

The work the student has done in the module is self assessed. Students are introduced to the idea gradually as the module progresses, by means of the schedules. There will be two or three interim attempts at self assessment, carefully structured, before the final assessment, which is fully described on the checklist. They may choose for themselves how they want to be assessed from a range of modes and are encouraged to choose more than one mode to be assessed on. Assessment can be written or spoken or an artifact – or a mixture of the three. These can be negotiated. Self assessment is broken up to make the tasks manageable. The students grade themselves on a pro-forma under three headings:

- Targets achieved

- Organisation

- Skills developed.

A co-ordinator or other appropriate person externally assesses the student's work and the student's self assessment and responds in writing to the student. They may agree with the student or can moderate the student's self-awarded grade up or down provided they have a reason. Students can come back on this. Those at risk of failure get an automatic interview. They cannot re-take the module.

Students are encouraged to work in pairs but they gain individual assessments because their checklist is individual to each person.

Evaluation
The terms of the contract are very clear. Co-ordinators try to make sure that all criteria for the running of the module and its assessment are open.

The majority of students feel that they learn a lot from the Open Module. They are in charge of their own learning and their own assessment, although difficult decisions can be discussed and negotiated. The weekly checklist keeps them with a safe boundary at what is, for the majority of students, an early stage in making their own important decisions. The least successful projects are those devolved to advisers who want to turn the open learning into a taught course.

Students learn that they must meet deadlines. In the first year of operation 12 students missed the deadline the first week. They all lost one grade point on whatever final grade they would get. After that there were no missed deadlines.

Surgeries could be theoretically from 2pm to 5pm every afternoon but this length of time has, up to now, never been found necessary. Co-ordinators fit the surgeries around labs.

Co-ordinators report that assessment by the students is remarkably accurate except for the extremes. It is low risk assessment, as they feel is right for this stage in the student's academic life. Although the marks count towards a student's final degree classification it comes at a point where it does not count very much or have much influence. However, failure to take the exercise seriously could be punitive because it could mean the student having to re-sit, i.e. if a student obtains an E grade there is an oral examination. If there are four fails in two years a student is asked to leave.

There has been a change in the module over three years: the details on the checklists have increased, as has their frequency. There is now a much tighter contract between the student and the co-ordinators. The co-ordinators feel this leaves much less room for misunderstanding on the part of the students as to what is expected of them.

Discussion

This module, like all others in the School, is routinely evaluated by the students at the end of the term. It has consistently received high praise from a majority of the students for the learning they feel has taken place. There are comments from students who feel they have not achieved their own aims but that, even so, they have learned a great deal about themselves. Many of them ask to do more work like this.

The co-ordinators agree that, although it is good to have experienced staff to co-ordinate the Open Module, the most important thing is that they are enthusiastic, both for the idea and for what the students wish to attempt.

They also feel that there could be difficulties in finding enough willing specialists to help students, both within and without the department. Co-ordinators could spend a lot of time trying to locate these specialists. The co-ordinators report that much of the work in running the Open Module is involved with record keeping.

Bibliography

Brookfield, D. ed, (1985), *Self-directed learning: from theory to practice*, New Directions for Continuing Education, No. 25, San Fransisco: Jossey-Bass

Baume, D. and S. Brown, eds, (1992), *Learning contracts*. Volume 2: Some practical examples, Paper 72, Birmingham: Staff and Educational Development Association

Boud, D. (1992), 'The use of self-assessment schedules in relation to negotiated learning', *Studies in Higher Education*, 17, 2, pp. 185-200

Brown, S. and D. Baume, eds, (1992), *Learning contracts*. Volume 1: A Theoretical Perspective, Paper 71, Birmingham: Staff and Educational Development Association

Cork, A. (1993), *Learning contracts*. Self Study Packs Series: De Montfort University

Knowles, M. S. (1986), *Using learning contracts: practical approaches to individualising and structuring learning*, San Fransisco: Jossey Bass

McCarthy, M. (1991), 'Factors affecting negotiation', *Journal for Further and Higher Education*, 15, 1

Robertson, C. (1992), *Work-Based learning Contracts*, Sheffield: Employment Department Group

Stephenson, J. and M. Laycock, eds, (1993), *Using Learning Contracts in Higher Education*, London: Kogan Page

Tomkins, C. and M. J. McGraw, (1988), 'The negotiated learning contract', in D. Boud, ed, *Developing Student Autonomy in Learning*, London: Kogan Page

7 Using Self and Peer Assessment

Introduction

Self and peer assessment involves students judging the quality of their own or of other students' work or performance. It may involve giving feedback, marking or both. Peer feedback may be used as an input to self assessment. It is used for a variety of reasons:

- to develop students' judgment. The best way for students to learn about what quality consists of, in an essay, presentation or whatever, is through practising making judgments and gradually calibrating these judgments against those of others, especially those of an expert such as a tutor;

- to enable students to supervise their own work. Once students have developed their judgment they can start to make decisions about where errors or weaknesses are, about which aspects of their work need improving and about what improvements might be made. This then improves the quality of students' work;

- to involve students' responsibly in their learning so that they are thinking about criteria and outcomes from the start and are more likely to check their own work carefully and thoughtfully rather than leaving all assessment up to the tutor;

- to engage students in talking to other students about their work. Peer assessment can lead to students giving detailed explanations of strengths and weaknesses in others' work and to peer-tutoring, involving correcting mistakes and improving work;

- to save tutors' time. Not all self and peer assessment processes save tutor's marking time but useful savings can be made if this is important.

Practical matters

Self and peer assessment takes several forms, not all of which involve allocating marks:

Self-assessment sheets

These are proforma students complete about their own work when they submit it for assessment by a tutor. The sheets are simply attached to their essay, report or whatever and are considered part of the assignment: without the completed self-assessment sheet the work is considered incomplete and referred back to the student. They are intended to encourage students to be more self-critical and to check their work more carefully. Initially, these sheets might be quite structured to give students ideas about the kinds of things they should be reviewing. This structure might include criteria and rating scales as well as headings for self-assessment comments. The proforma might be specific to each type of assignment: for example, employing different sheets for essays, reports, lab reports etc. Over time the criteria might be negotiated with students and the sheets might include more open-ended headings used such as:

- What are the strongest features of your work?

- What additional work would you have to do to get one grade higher than the grade you are going to get?

Students might eventually be asked to suggest a grade and to justify this grade by reviewing the strengths and weaknesses of the assignment. However, none of this need involve students actually awarding themselves marks which count towards the formal assessment system.

Peer assessment using mark sheets or model answers

Here students are used as substitute tutors. If the type of assignment allows it, for example, with calculations or work which can be clearly correct or incorrect, marking sheets may provide enough guidance for students to mark as accurately as tutors can. Model answers or model laboratory reports, together with guidance, can also enable students to mark with acceptable levels of reliability. Monitoring is necessary to ensure rigorous and fair marking but savings in tutor's time are still possible. The School of Pharmacy at Leeds University dramatically reduced marking time for lab reports while improving the quality of students' lab reports (as judged by independent tutors) by using peer assessment leading to marks supported by marking sheets. This is probably the largest single category of use of self and peer assessment and techniques for controlling and monitoring it, and producing reliable marks at low cost are well developed.

Self assessment leading to marks

Here students award themselves marks. The use of clear criteria and rating scales can lead to acceptable reliability, as can training in assessment which improves the quality of students' judgment. Inexperienced students may over-estimate their marks while more sophisticated students may underestimate their marks. Monitoring is necessary and tutors may need to retain the right to moderate marks. Savings in tutors' time may be difficult to achieve if monitoring is done adequately.

Peer assessment of open-ended assignments

Here peers are used to judge the quality of assignments. Where marking is relatively subjective and based on judgment rather than mark sheets, students' marking is likely to be less reliable and peer assessment tends to be less reliable than self assessment.

Peer feedback as an input to self assessment

Peer assessment may be most useful as feedback to students rather than to provide marks. In particular it may be useful for students to gain peer feedback before writing the final draft of an assignment, or as an input to self assessment, whether or not this involves marks: a case study below describes the use of peer input to self assessment on a counselling course.

Peer assessment within groups

In some situations the only people in a position to make valid judgments about a student's work are other students. For example, in tutor-less seminar groups the seminar group members are in the best position to assess the quality of a seminar presentation. And in group project work the students are usually in the best position to assess the relative contribution of each of the other members of the group. Here, although there may still be problems with reliability and fairness, the students' judgments may be the best available.

Key Issues

There are many potential pitfalls with self assessment and especially with peer assessment. The key issues include:

Why is self or peer assessment being used?

Is the assessment designed to increase students' commitment to their assignment? Is it designed primarily to develop students' judgment and ability to self-assess? Is it intended to save tutor's marking time? If it is being used primarily to support learning then it may not help to have the marks counting towards the formal assessment system.

What can students validly judge?

Students may be in a good position to judge if a seminar presentation is 'lively' or 'clear', but are they able to judge if the presentation involves a 'good breadth of knowledge'? It is important to recognise what students can and cannot validly judge if their feedback or marks are to be reliable and useful.

What criteria are involved?

Students' judgment will not, initially, be very sophisticated. Without guidance concerning the criteria you want them to use they may be swayed by surface features and not consider crucial aspects. Criteria need to be explicit and clear.

Simple labels, such as 'use of sources' may provide little useful guidance, and what such a criterion means is likely to need explaining, preferably with good and bad examples for each criterion. Rating scales should have both ends of the scale described. Where criteria are described in the form of clear rating scales there is a temptation to use the scales to allocate marks. However the overall quality of a piece of work is seldom simply the sum of its parts and the mark obtained by adding marks against criteria may produce a surprising overall mark. The rigid use of rating scales, especially when used by students, tends to produce both different means and different ranges of marks than do global judgments made after the rating scales have been used for guidance.

Where should the criteria come from?

Initially it may be sensible to use the tutor's criteria, especially where there are criteria which are regularly used in assessment, such as a standard set of essay marking criteria used across a whole department. Students may initially find tutor's criteria difficult to use and may need to spend some time understanding the tutor's language and operationalising it into concrete examples of features of different standards. With experience, students will be in a position to contribute to criteria, negotiate criteria or even propose their own set. If you are worried about reliability and validity then keep control of at least some of the criteria. If you intend to allow different students or different groups to use different criteria then be clear in your own mind that the advantages in terms of student commitment and understanding gained from this outweigh the losses of reliability and comparability which will result.

How do students develop judgment?

Students do not start off with sophisticated, valid or reliable judgment. You cannot expect them to do a worthwhile job, and certainly not expect them to produce meaningful marks, without some practice and training. Effective training exercises include:

- getting all students to mark a moderate piece of work and discussing the features everyone thinks are good and bad and the marks everyone gives, and why they give them;

- marking work and comparing marks and comments with those of the tutor;

- completing self-assessment sheets and comparing these comments with the tutor's comments;

- using peer assessment for feedback prior to self assessment;

- practising using a given set of criteria or rating scales to produce a consensus on ratings and marks within a group for a sample of work.

Do students object?

Students often believe that it is a tutor's job to assess work, either because 'that's what they are paid for' or because they don't trust their own inexpert judgment or the judgment of their colleagues. If no effort is made to explain the educational rationale for self and peer assessment students are unlikely to be convinced. And if you tell them that they are as able as you to mark work or that their judgments are as valid as yours, without any prior training, they will be justifiably sceptical. You are also likely to have to explain how your system avoids unfairness and cheating. Students are right to be suspicious and it is the tutor's responsibility to reassure them by careful explanation of the steps which have been taken to avoid pitfalls. In general, it is sensible to give students at least one 'dummy run' using self or peer assessment before any marks count towards qualifications.

Do students make reliable markers?

Students can learn to self assess as reliably as tutor's colleagues, given guidance and training. Peer assessment tends to be a little less reliable. The reliability of both self and peer assessment is likely to depend to some extent on the nature of the culture it is being used within. If competitiveness and cheating is common this will obviously influence marks differently than if co-operation and honesty is the norm. The more open-ended the assessment task and the more subjective the judgments involved, the less reliable students' judgments are likely to be. However, tutor's marking also tends to be highly unreliable in these circumstances and a modest additional loss of reliability may be a small price to pay for the potential learning gains.

Does self and peer assessment produce acceptable means and ranges of marks?

The mean marks produced by self assessment have been found to be lower than tutor's marks in some contexts and higher in others. Unsophisticated students tend to over-estimate grades while more sophisticated or experienced students tend to underestimate grades, compared with their tutors' judgments.

Students may be reluctant to award very high or very low marks, partly out of lack of confidence in their own judgment, and the resulting range of marks may be narrow. Where rating scales are used to allocate marks against criteria without the extremes of the scales being labelled, students seem particularly reluctant to use the extremes of the scales and the range of marks this produces can be very narrow. With peer assessment, if you average the marks allocated by a number of peers to an individual piece of work, in an attempt to increase reliability, this tends to produce a narrow range of marks overall and poor discrimination between students.

Do marks count towards the formal assessment system?

Given the potential for problems it is often sensible to limit the proportion of total marks which come from self or peer assessment on a course , unless there is potential for tutor moderation of marks. It is also sensible to give students some practice with self and peer assessment where the marks do not count, before doing it 'for real'.

What safeguards are there?

What is to stop students marking themselves up? In practice this tends not to happen and there is often more danger of students recognising weaknesses more easily than strengths and marking themselves a little harshly. But if there is the potential for deliberate over-estimation of marks then there should be some monitoring and the tutor should have the final decision. If the tutor regularly moderates students' marks this will undermine the whole exercise and indicate that students need more training to improve their judgment. With peer assessment there is more scope for unfairness and even victimisation. It can be possible to anonymise assignments so that students do not know which student's work they are marking, and to sample a proportion to check that problems are not occurring. Except with relatively short pieces of work which can be marked quickly using marking schemes this monitoring may be very time-consuming.

How are disputes handled?

There should be clear procedures for handling situations where a student's self-assessment mark is well above what the tutor thinks appropriate or where a peer-assessed mark is lower than a student thinks fair and also where a peer-assessment mark is higher than a tutor thinks reasonable. The simplest ground rule (and one that is usually acceptable to Examinations' Committees but which may undermine students' commitment to self and peer assessment) is that all marks may be moderated by the tutor. Without adequate safeguards and clear dispute procedures students may not be happy about peer assessment.

What documentation is involved?

Where possible the way the assessment operates should be written down clearly, including a rational, full descriptions of criteria to be used, proforma and outlines of safeguards. Students should be able to refer to criteria while they are working on their assignments, and not just at the point they are being asked to assess work.

What evidence can external examiners see?

Students' self- or peer-assessment comments, ratings and marks should be available to external examiners to the same extent as tutor's comments and marks. This may involve photocopies of completed proforma or other record-keeping. If students assess work of a transitory nature, such as a seminar presentation, then samples of seminars of varying quality should be video- or audio-recorded so that the examiners can see the relationship between students' judgments and their own. This may only be necessary the first time the system operates so as to satisfy the examiners regarding standards. Discuss your assessment scheme with your externals at the time you design it and seek advice.

Case Studies

Negotiation and Peer Assessment on a Science Education Course

Trevor Habeshaw, Technical and Educational Services Ltd

Innovator: Jo Corke, University of the West of England

Course Context

On a full-time course in professional teacher training for students specialising in Primary Science, because of school experience demands the timetable is blocked into days and half days of teaching so the students have long periods together. There are 20 students in the group. About two thirds have Biology 'A' level and most of them are 18-year-old entrants. The rest of the students have a variety of entrants qualifications Access, SRN, 'A' level Human Biology but no 'A' level Biology.

The BEd course documentation states that there will be an element of negotiation in the assessment which will increase as the course progresses. Negotiation is defined as a dialogue between tutor and students which allows the students to be involved actively in selecting topics, and identifying criteria by which particular assignments are marked. The peer assessment processes described below have been carried out since the degree was initially validated in 1985.

Students are introduced to peer assessment in year 1 where they can practice peer marking of projects. These marks do not contribute to students' final degree classifications but do contribute to pass/fail decisions about progressing to year 2.

This peer marking described here replaced a tutor-marked project which was both repetitive and time consuming to mark. Now all written feedback comments are made by the students. The tutor still sees all the projects, mainly to moderate this feedback but also because the students like her to be involved. As a result the students see a range of work, some of it better than the work they have produced themselves (as judged by final grades awarded) and, with the help of the criteria selected, have a chance to examine it more critically than if they had simply followed the instruction: 'Look at the work of someone else who got a better mark and see how it could be done' which seems too vague and unproductive.

Assessment

Clarification of assessment objectives for the project is achieved through discussions about the criteria and their specific weightings. Students are instructed in using the criteria which involves both discussion and practice. Each year students decide which criteria are to be used to assess the projects, drawing on a 'menu' supplied by the tutor, and what weightings the different criteria shall have, as in the example overleaf.

During the discussion they are told that the external examiner will want to see, and discuss with the markers, those assignments which are graded 1A or 3C. The grading scheme is supplied by the tutor and focusses on the way in which criteria – whatever they have been negotiated to include – are met.

A year-2 project involves students analysing personal diet records. The project marking takes place in a three hour period and involves the following stages.

1.   The class is divided into two groups. Each group is allocated its own room and half the projects. Group A takes group B's projects and vice versa so that no students are marking their own projects.

2.   The criteria are reviewed and 30 minutes browsing time is allowed in which students get a general feel for the projects.

3.   They then have 90 minutes in which they each mark some of the projects. In this time each student marks, on average, about three projects.

4.   When the time is up, the several marks for each project are then aggregated and a simple average score is produced. The score is then compared against criteria laid down in the BEd submission document for classification purposes. Sometimes students appoint a moderator to ensure equal treatment across markers and classifications.

5   The finalised marks are presented to the tutor who moderates the peer assessment, especially where it is possible that a poor student may not be sufficiently aware of the standards required and may over-mark a mediocre student's work because she/he could not understand the technical content.

Discussion

The External Examiner was wary of the peer assessment process from the start. He wanted the tutor to justify putting the students through this process. His second concern focussed on the issue of students' competence to make evaluations of one anothers' work. At first he asked to see all scripts but is now satisfied enough only to sample each year.

The tutor wanted the students to experience the responsibility associated with judgment of the work of other human beings. While she is sure that the exercise does not reduce stress at the time of the activity, students say they come to appreciate how criteria are devised and that they can more easily see how to fulfil the criteria in later work.

The tutor is quite satisfied that the students are capable of assessing their colleagues' work, following the training. Peer assessment makes them take care over the task because at the end they have to justify the marks to their classmates. The number of firsts and thirds awarded is not noticeably different from those assessments which are only marked by tutors. Furthermore, peer assessment offers a number of other useful benefits for trainee teachers in that it requires them to have a good understanding of what is being assessed and a clear mechanism for assessing it, and to be aware of the importance of deadlines if they are sharing data. All this is useful training for their future careers.

The tutor believes that for this process to be copied elsewhere the following issues should be borne in mind:

- there should be detailed instructions and discussion of the process beforehand;

- the practice run should take place on an activity which 'counts';

- the topic chosen for the study should be new to the students so that some members of the group do not have an unfair advantage;

- there should be no free choice with the topic (at least to start with) as this makes comparisons between students easier;

- separating the doing from the marking seems to enable the marking to be undertaken in a calmer atmosphere, so the project report should be handed in a week beforehand.

Peer Assessed Project in Nutrition

The project will be peer assessed on 03.12.91. Non-attendance on this date will mean that your project is not marked. We have agreed the following criteria:

(10)   Presentation

(1)   .....   Is it presented on time?

(3)   .....   Is it passable prose?

(3)   .....   Is it a pleasure to read?

(3)   .....   Is it legible, well laid out and well designed?

(20)   Approach

(5)   .....   Is the level suitable for the audience?

(5)   .....   Does it challenge the reader?

(5)   .....   Does it cover the range and scope that the title suggests?

(5)   .....   Does it extend the reader into new areas of concern?

(70)   Content and Comment *With reference to the learning objectives does it:*

(10)   .....   Select from the material available that which is relevant?

(10)   .....   Identify strengths and weaknesses in the data/material?

(10)   .....   Attempt unbiased criticism of the material?

(10)   .....   Bring to the reader's attention other evidence to support or discredit these criticisms?

(10)   .....   Give adequate information (& references of same) to enable the reader to form her or his own judgments?

(10)   .....   Summarise the information and comments to give the reader some guidance?

(10)   .....   Spare

Total

(100)   .....

Self and Peer Assessment on a Counselling Skills Course

Trevor Habeshaw, Technical and Educational Services Ltd

Innovator: Sue Habeshaw, Department of Humanities,
University of the West of England

Course Context

This is a part-time evening, Level 1 Certificate course, designed as an initial training course for counsellors from a variety of settings, and approved by the University as part of its modular degree proposal. The year group consists of 24 students who meet for 125 hours which involves two weekends followed by 30 three-hour sessions.

The whole of this course is student centred in that students are provided with a variety of structures and frameworks into which they import almost all of the content, and determine a large part of the assessment.

Description of Assessment

The assessment regime for the course comprises eight items of which five are written pieces and the other three are self-, peer- and tutor-assessed practical work. Assessment is on a pass/fail basis and students must gain a pass on all the assessment items in order to pass the course.

Formative, oral self and peer assessment by members of the student group takes place throughout the course during reflection sessions which are built into the weekly training exercises. The exercises are normally conducted in groups of three with each person taking turns as counsellor, client and observer. The feedback regime included in these exercises requires the Counsellor in each part of the exercise to give himself or herself feedback first before receiving feedback from the Client and the Observer. In addition, students are expected to make notes after the session in order to monitor their progress and accumulate data which they can use in their assignments and in the self- and peer-assessment exercise.

The students are prepared for the written self- and peer-assessment exercise by the use of an interim Self and Peer Report. Ultimately they undertake a final self and peer assessment (both written and verbal), which is run as a group activity over a period of nine hours and for which they are wholly responsible.

The Interim Self and Peer Report

The interim report consists of a three-page printed form which contains all the instructions for the activity.

1. Students read instructions in respect of the criteria they are using in their initial self assessment. If the exercise is to be completed during a

single session of two hours, 15 minutes should be allowed for thinking and writing time. Students can be asked to complete this stage in their own time and take as long over this as they wish.

2.   All the reports are piled on a convenient table and, in their own time, each person takes another student's report, reads the self-assessment and, noting the criteria used and bearing in mind any specific requests for feedback that might have been made, writes a peer assessment on the second page, signing their name when they have done so.

They then place the report back on the table, select another one, read through what has been written on the report so far, and add their own comments.

This process is repeated until either everyone has written on everyone else's report form, or the time allowed for this part of the activity has run out. Most reports will have about ten comments on them by the end of this time. Students are given at least an hour for this stage.

3.   Individuals then retrieve their own report from the pile and read through their own and then through other people's comments. When they are ready to do so they then write a second version of their self-report bearing in mind, and reflecting, the extent that they wish to do so, the comments of their peers.

4.   Individuals decide how they want the final self-report to be used.

The Appendices contain the instructions and briefing students are given on how to use the self- and peer-assessment form and the headings used on the form.

Evaluation

This type of self and peer assessment has been run since the course began and five intakes of students have experienced and evaluated it. They have not found it an easy task and yet each year students have consistently reported it as being one of the most valuable learning experiences of the course. The test of the ability of the students to carry this through came in both the second and fourth year of the course, when two students were failed in the peer-assessment procedure.

The staff believe that the process is working well, primarily because the students take it very seriously, and because they have always agreed with the students' decisions. This success has not come about by chance but from the care taken in the course design to introduce the idea of self and peer assessment right from the start, and to train and support students in its implementation.

Because the self and peer assessment on this course 'counts' and represents 25% of the final assessment of the course, those responsible for the institutional monitoring and review procedure have taken a special interest in it. The annual Course Report, including the outcomes of the self- and peer-assessment procedure, has been carefully scrutinised and accepted. In addition to seeing all the formal written assignments the External Examiner has approved and supported the self- and peer-assessment procedure.

Discussion

From the first meeting of the course, and then throughout the programme, students are the primary givers of formative feedback to their peers. The staff circulate and observe everyone during the course of the year. But the students themselves are the most frequent observers of their peers and as such are in the best position to give feedback. Counsellors are often in the position of giving feedback to their clients. Consequently, it is of great importance that they develop their skills of giving (and receiving) authentic feedback. Even if they are in receipt of regular and effective supervision, counsellors almost always work on their own. It is therefore of great importance that they develop their self-assessment skills to a high level and their confidence in these skills.

The structured regime of self- and peer-assessment described here trains students in the skills of assessment, encourages them to practise these skills in advance and expects them then to use the skills in a meaningful setting. Students must pass the self and peer assessment in order to pass the course. This conveys to the students the extent to which the course team genuinely values the contribution that students can make to the assessment process.

Appendix A

**UNIVERSITY OF THE WEST OF ENGLAND
CERTIFICATE IN COUNSELLING SKILLS
SELF AND PEER ASSESSMENT**

The task
For the self and peer final assessment of this course you are expected:
(a) to give feedback to yourself and toothers on your skills, abilities and
    potential as counsellors. This can be based on your observation of a
    counselling session and/or anything relevant tyou have noticed
    about the person in the group or elsewhere;
(b) to assess yourselves and others as counsellors on a pass/referred
    basis.

Taking the task seriously
Remember that you have a responsibility only to pass group members
about whom you are confident. It is better that people who, in your
personal opinion, are not good enough, should be referred at this stage
and given the chance to improve.

Doing the self and peer assessment
• You can do this in any way you like providing you all agree to it and
  that the available time is shared fairly.
• Agree criteria or not, as you prefer.
• Take coffee breaks when you like and, if you want to, take time for
  review, relaxation or games.

The programme
Three sessions have been set aside for the self, peer and course
assessment. Please give the course leader a list of results of the self and
peer assessment by 8 30pm on the 27th of June. Please allow the half
hour between 8 30 and 9 00 on the 27th of June for the course
assessment. As many of the tutors who can will join you for this.

The role of the tutors
Tutors will be available on the 13th, 20th and 27th of June. We will be
happy to give advice, information, support etc., if asked. You can invite
us to join the group or consult us in Room 10.

Appendix B

Self & Peer Assessment Form

These sheets provide you with an opportunity to prepare for the self and peer assessment activity, in which you will be asked to make a public assessment of yourself and of your peers, and which concludes this course.

Self assessment
Your name is included on the attached form. Think of the times you have worked as counsellor during the Co-counselling, the Bridging Course, the 6 Category Intervention Analysis, and the Rogerian and Gestalt Approaches to Counselling elements. Assess yourself using the same procedures as for the peer assessment. Continue on a separate sheet if you want to.

Peer assessment
As you work for the rest of the year in pairs or three's, as client or observer, with other members of the group, evaluate them as counsellors as far as your experience of them allows.

The procedures for giving feedback are written out in full in the Introduction to Counselling booklet. You could start by completing the following sentences:

One good thing she/he did as counsellor was ....
One way I would have liked her/him to be different as counsellor was ....

Write as much as you want to about each person and continue on a separate sheet if necessary.

Appendix C

Certificate in Counselling Skills: Self & Peer Report (Final)
In the space below write a report for yourself as a member of this course. Note below the criteria you are using in your self assessment. Use the third person (she/he rather than I) and include equal mention of your good qualities as well as your limitations. List any specific aspects about which you would like to receive feedback from others in the spaces on page 2.

Name

                              Date

Criteria
-                                     •
-                                     •
-                                     •

Special requests for feedback
In addition to your own feedback, please give me feedback about the following matters

-                             •
-                             •
-                             •
-                             •

INSTRUCTIONS
In the space below, write some feedback to the person named on page 1 taking into account any criteria and any particular requests. Try to offer constructive criticism as well as praise. It's helpful if you sign your name in case the person wants to check anything out with you.

Read the comments on page 2.
Decide how you want to alter your report in the light of what others have written about you.
Write an amended version in the space below.

PLEASE TICK ONE OF THE FOLLOWING

I agree to this entire document being included in my personal file   ☐

I will produce an agreed summary of this document to be included in my personal file   ☐

Signed   Date

Peer assessment of engineering problems using marking schemes

Graham Gibbs

Innovators: D. Forbes and J. Spence, Department of Mechanical Engineering, University of Strathclyde

Course Context

On a large 2nd-year Mechanical Engineering course students were expected to undertake a substantial number of problems on tutorial sheets on a regular basis. In practice many students did not undertake the problems or attend the tutorials. It was not possible to mark these tutorial problems due to the marking load associated with 170 students and students were not penalised for not having tackled them. As a result the mid-term examinations revealed very poor performance with an average of 51% and as many as a third of students obtaining less than 35%. This should have indicated to the student that they needed to undertake more of the tutorial work, but while the end of course exams produced higher marks they were still poor overall and students struggled to redeem the situation. The two exams involved a substantial marking load but this marking failed to elicit appropriate learning behaviour and led to poor performance.

Assessment

In the redesigned course students were required to complete 60 problems during the course. Each of six units of work was accompanied by a series of tutorial problems and a tutor-marked 'degree standard' problem. In all, 15 problem sheets containing a total of 120 problems were handed out to students. By a set date at the end of each Unit students had to complete the 'degree standard' problem and 40% of the tutorial problems correctly completed. Late submission of solutions was severely penalised.

At the end of each Unit there was peer assessment in class using model answers. Students in alternate rows swapped solutions and marked the work in front of them as the tutor worked through correct solutions on the board using a standard 'marking solution' of which all students were given a copy. 60% of students' marks came from the problems and 40% from the mid-term exam unless insufficient correct problems were submitted during the Units, in which case a final exam was employed. Successful completion of the six Units exempted students from the final exam.

Evaluation

There was no change in the content, pace or order of the material taught but students' mid-term exam score increased markedly, from an average of 51% to an average of 76% with almost no failures. Students learnt to peer assess with increasing speed and competence, reducing marking time from about 40 minutes down to seven minutes. As almost all students completed sufficient problems successfully very few were required to take the final exam, so saving marking time.

The success was attributed to:

- the students having completed far more tutorial problems than previously;

- the students seeing preferred solutions with mark weightings together with other students' work which required careful analysis and judgment to mark. This led to them structuring their own work more appropriately in future.

Whether students collaborated on problems or whether peer marking was reliable here was not particularly important because the mid-point exam revealed such a large increase in performance. Collaboration could have improved understanding. Here the effect of peer assessment is largely formative. Through the requirement to complete work, regular feedback and analysis of requirements and of correct solutions, students changed their study habits and this produced improved performance on conventional, tutor-marked assessments. There is no need in such circumstances to have elaborate control over students' marking behaviour or checks on their reliability.

Bibliography

Benett, Y. (1993), 'The Validity and Reliability of Assessments and Self-assessments of Work-based Learning', *Assessment and Evaluation in Higher Education*, 18, 2, pp. 83-94

Boekaerts, M. (1991), 'Subjective competence, appraisals and self-assessment', *Learning and Instruction*, 1, pp. 1-17

Boud, D. J. (1986), *Implementing Student Self Assessment*, Green Guide: 5. Sydney: Higher Education Research and Development Society of Australasia

Boud, D. (1989), 'The role of self assessment in student grading', *Assessment and Evaluation in Higher Education*, 14,1, pp. 20-30

Boud, D. and N. J. Falchikov, (1989), 'Quantitative studies of student self-assessment in higher education: a critical analysis of findings', *Higher Education*, 18, pp. 529-49

Boud, D. and W. H. Holmes, (1981), 'Self and peer marking in an undergraduate engineering course', *IEEE Transactions on Education*, E-24, 4, pp. 267-74

Boud, D., A. E. Churches and E. M. Smith, (1986), 'Student self-assessment in an engineering design course: an evaluation', *International Journal of Applied Engineering Education*, 2, 2, pp. 83-90

Boyd, H. and J. Cowan, (1985), 'A case for self-assessment based on recent studies of student learning', *Assessment and Evaluation in Higher Education*, 10, pp. 225-35

Brown, S. and P. Dove, eds, (1990), *Self and Peer Assessment in Higher Education*, Staff and Educational Development Association, Paper No. 63, Birmingham

Calhoun, J. G., D. J. Ten Haken, and J. O. Wooliscroft, (1990), 'Medical students' development of self- and peer-assessment skills: a longitudinal study', *Teaching and Learning in Medicine*, 2, pp. 25-9

Edwards, R. (1989), 'An experiment in student self-assessment', *British Journal of Educational Technology*, 20, pp. 5-10

Falchikov, J. N. and D. Boud, (1989), 'Student Self-Assessment in Higher Education: a meta-analysis', *Review of Educational Research*, 59: 4, pp. 395-430

Forbes, D. A. and J. Spence, (1991), 'An experiment in assessment for a large group', in R. A. Smith, ed, *Innovative Teaching in Engineering*, London: Ellis Horwood

King, W. and T. G. F. Gray, (1991), 'Peer marking of student reports', in R. A. Smith, ed, *Innovative Teaching in Engineering*, London: Ellis Horwood

King, W., P. F. Gray and J. D. W. Hossack, (1992), 'Peer marking of technical reports', *CAP-ability*, 2, pp. 20-5

Orpen, C. (1982), 'Student versus Lecturer Assessment of Learning: A Research Note', *Higher Education*, 11, 5, pp. 567-72

Schram, R. M. and G. E. Rich, (1990), 'Peer evaluation: is it a reliable method for grading oral presentations?' *Business Education Forum*, 44, p. 36

Siders, J. A. (1983), 'Instructor, Self and Peer Review: A Formative Evaluation Triad', *College Student Journal*, 17, 2, pp. 141-4

Stanton, H. (1978), 'Self-grading as an assessment method', *Improving College and University Teaching*, 26, 4, pp. 236-8

Woods, D. R., R. R. Marshall, and A. N. Hyrmak, (1988), 'Self assessment in the context of the McMaster problem-solving programme', *Assessment and Evaluation in Higher Education*, 13, pp. 107-27

Yarborough, C. (1987), 'The relationship of behavioural self-assessment to the achievement of basic conducting skills', *Journal of Research in Music Education*, 35, pp. 183-90

8 Using Profiles

Introduction

Profiles and profiling are becoming common, especially in vocational courses, but also increasingly in academic courses where progressive development of individual students and their skills is involved. It is a confusing area because so many different forms of profiling exist, each designed to achieve quite different things. As with most student centred methods there is a full range from highly-controlled frameworks with pre-specified learning outcomes to negotiated and open-ended frameworks with highly personalised outcomes. Profiles are used to:

- assess the achievement of a range of learning outcomes specified by a course, in order to produce a profile of achievement instead of a single grade or mark;

- assess transferable skills in parallel with course content, often using criteria and rating scales for each skill, whether or not this contributes to the formal assessment;

- provide a competency structure within which projects are negotiated and assessed;

- collate documentary evidence of various kinds, over a period of time, including records of non-academic learning which would normally be excluded, which together form a record of achievement of a qualitatively rich kind but which would be difficult to quantify;

- assess prior learning of such varied kinds that it does not lend itself to simple testing, in order to make appropriate course decisions or to accredit prior learning and provide exemptions from components of courses;

- provide records or assessments of work-based learning where evidence of experience and achievement is inevitably varied in form and often validated by a work-based supervisor rather than a tutor;

- help individuals to review and track their personal and professional development, outside of, or in parallel with, individual courses, and to prepare for careers, often through formative self assessment within a very open-ended framework.

Practical matters

In practice, much of profiling doesn't actually involve assessment, it is merely a framework within which assessment is undertaken and documented. Profiling of skills or competencies requires that students are set assignments which involve use of these skills and competencies and the assessment of these skills. This is tackled in chapter 5, Assessing Skills and Competencies. Profiles which collate evidence in portfolios still require a way of selecting and assessing the evidence. This is tackled in chapter 9, Using Portfolios. Personal profiling often involves the setting of personal targets and the rigorous review of these at a later date, and this is tackled in Chapter 6, Using Learning Contracts and Negotiated Assignments.

As the types of profiles are so varied, practical matters will be summarised for each type of use.

Assessment of course outcomes

Normally a list of learning outcomes is accompanied by associated rating scales representing levels of achievement of each. The profile represents an overview of levels of achievement of each outcome. Some scales involve degrees of excellence only e.g. Unsatisfactory; Adequate; Good; Excellent, and, because no definition of 'satisfactory' is provided this makes it very difficult to judge when an outcome has been satisfactorily achieved. Some scales go into more detail on what behaviour might be expected at each level. Other scales relate to experience, e.g. Not yet encountered; Observed; Undertaken under supervision; Undertaken alone; Undertaken in a wide variety of settings. Such scales are much easier to use but clearly relate to a particular definition of outcome.

The problem is how to produce sufficiently-clear specification of learning outcomes, and associated criteria and standards, to make assessment possible and manageable. Writing useful learning outcomes is very difficult. Devising an appropriate assessment for each outcome can be daunting and often leads to excessive assessment loads. In practice, one assignment may be used to provide evidence relating to several outcomes.

Combining individual assessments of outcomes into a profile also confronts assessors with the problem of determining how many outcomes can be left out or only partially achieved with the student still considered to have 'passed' or, in some cases, achieved a 'distinction' or even a mark. As has become clear in the press concerning the assessment of NVQs, the use of detailed profiles does not necessarily ensure evenness of standards.

Assessment of transferable skills

Outside the assessment of NVQs, the use of profiles in higher education is most commonly associated with transferable skills. In some institutions (such as Oxford Brookes University), the use of profiles of transferable skills is now universal, within an institution-wide lists of skills and every student leaving with a profile, but with discipline-based variations in definitions of skills and local variations in implementation.

Profiling is often separate from the assessment, which may take place within written assignments, seminar presentations, group projects or whatever, and is undertaken as a summary of evidence provided by other sources or even as a subjective reflective review based on a wide variety of learning experiences which may not have been specifically designed to contribute to profiling.

Profiling often relies on students' self-assessment, perhaps influenced by peer feedback but is only lightly moderated by tutors because they do not have the time to assess students themselves. Nor do the tutors know the students well enough to make sound judgments about the personal qualities they have demonstrated in modules with which they themselves are quite unfamiliar. Such profiles cannot easily carry the same weight of institutional certification of standards that degree classifications have without equivalent effort and resources involved in double marking, external examining and so on. As with so many aspects of student centred assessment it is therefore often best seen as a formative device supporting learning rather than as a summative device which can reliably indicate outcomes.

Profiles used in this way may relate to an individual module or, more commonly, to an entire degree programme. Some profiling schemes focus on different sub-sets of skills at different stages: for example, academic study skills in year 1, discipline-related transferable skills in year 2, and work-related transferable skills in year 3. In modular programmes where there is no institutional policy, it is not uncommon for students to be involved in trying to work with several different and incompatible profiling systems containing different skills, different definitions and different processes.

Records of achievement

The use of records of achievement is now almost universal in schools. Many of the practical issues for higher education are the same as those in chapter 9, Using Portfolios, i.e., specifying the types of evidence which are appropriate to include; providing a rationale and criteria which enable decisions about selection and inclusion to be made; briefing students on how to build up their records of achievement; reviewing the record from time to time, and encouraging self and peer review, in order to set targets for the collation of further evidence over an extended period of time and so on.

Unlike portfolios, however, most records of achievement are not summatively assessed by tutors and are not associated with individual modules, but are kept by students to show to employers after their studies are complete. Not having to judge or grade them solves a problem for the tutor but causes another for the student and for the employer. In the absence of a grade or other shorthand for relative quality of outcomes, records of achievement need to be easily and quickly interpretable by non-specialists. This means they have to be reasonably short, well organised and signposted, possibly with interpretive statements or commentaries, so as to make the significance of evidence clearer. In the end, however, the evidence largely has to stand for itself. And it has to look credible, which means the sources have to be selected carefully. Records of achievement have not yet established themselves as a regular component in graduate recruitment: they are often too bulky to send by post and too varied to allow easy comparison of applicants. They can, however, provide a valuable framework within which students can seek and evaluate the benefit of a wide range of learning opportunities and it is this learning function which ought to be the primary focus of attention. Records of Achievement can nevertheless still be used as a resource to respond to specific requests for information from different potential employers.

Assessment of prior learning (APL)

APL takes many forms, some of which involve the framework of a profile to summarise past learning. Competence-based Certificate in Management courses, for example, usually invite students to present evidence of past learning against the courses' list of competencies and tutors then negotiate with students both the form of evidence and the extent to which it represents adequacy. Here the profile may be the same as that used for assessment of outcomes from the course. Clear outcome statements, clear criteria and standards, clear ground rules for acceptable sources of evidence, and open discussion between tutors to standardise approaches seem vital. Variation between tutors can be even wider than that between essay markers. Students also need clear guidance and support in preparing evidence and making cases.

Records of work-based learning

Profiling is often used within work-based learning to clarify the purpose of the experience through specifying the desired learning outcomes or skills, to structure supervision and the negotiation of learning opportunities within the workplace, or the negotiation of learning contracts which may form the basis of assessment of the overall experience. Profiles may be used at several stages during a work placement to review progress and redirect the kinds of work undertaken and the focus of learning. They may involve a core set of unnegotiable outcomes or skills with scope for the addition of workplace-specific outcomes. Negotiation and review using the profile may involve a three-way discussion with the student an equal partner with the tutor and workplace supervisor. Sometimes students return from a work placement and then put together evidence in a profile in a similar way to bidding for exemptions through accreditation of prior learning.

Well-developed systems train and prepare both students and supervisors and use a profile as the framework which directs and holds together all aspects of an otherwise messy and poorly focussed experience, drawing out and documenting more learning.

Personal development and career orientation

This is often the most open-ended and forward-looking form of profiling. Sometimes the proforma associated with profiles for personal development are largely blank with short prompts such as 'What skills do you already have' or 'What skills do you want to acquire?', and some profiles consist of little more than a glossy folder with nothing in it! To make productive use of such frameworks often requires close tutorial support and plenty of discussion over a period of time. It usually involves group or workshop exercises to analyse past experience and skills, to set goals and to review their achievement. This may happen within a structured framework of defined skills and specified outcomes but is usually almost entirely negotiated and student driven. It is often associated with a first-year personal tutoring programme (as at the College of Ripon and York St. John) or runs alongside an entire degree. It is not common for it to operate within a taught and conventionally-assessed module, though some institutions, including the Open University, have credit-bearing profiling modules which are concerned with personal development and career preparation and planning. Sometimes it operates alongside self-contained elements of a professional programme (such as teacher training) and integrates course content with professional experience and development in a very personal way.

It is not common to use any summative assessment with such profiling as it is unclear what should be assessed. Would a student who was at a low starting point but who was good at setting targets and who developed well be worth a higher grade than a student who had better transferable skills at the outset and was good at writing self assessments but who did not exploit the potential of profiling for learning? Any formal assessment would have to have very explicit goals and any criteria such as 'quality of reflection' would have to be carefully defined and communicated to students. As with the use of reflective diaries, summative assessment can produce 'faking good' and instrumental approaches, undermining the whole purpose of the exercise.

Structuring negotiated project work

Profiling can be used as the framework within which project work is set up and assessed as an alternative to other ways of clarifying the purposes and criteria for project work (see chapter 4, Using Projects). Students can be allowed to negotiate whatever project they like provided they can show how it will embody a set of competencies. Students may be permitted to undertake several small projects which, between them, cover all the necessary competencies. Students may be allowed to specify what evidence will be produced through the project work as well as criteria for judging the adequacy of evidence for each competency.

Key Issues

Many of the key issues have been raised through describing practical matters or are addressed in the chapters on Skills, Contracts or Portfolios, so the following discussion is brief.

Why is profiling being used?

The educational rationale for profiling has to be particularly clear because this so clearly affects the form profiling should take. Assessing the achievement of specified competencies will require a completely different form than supporting personal development.

Will profiling contribute to formal assessment or is it largely formative in nature?

Much of the value of profiling is formative and the use of profiles to summatively assess outcomes or the production of documentation to summarise what has been learnt as a certified piece of evidence will make such heavy demands on the rigour of the process that it will be completely changed in nature. Using profiling as a developmental process and then summatively assessing the outcomes can cause problems of authenticity and validity of evidence, reliability of judgment and undermining of intrinsic motivation in students as well as being very time consuming.

How are individual competencies combined into a single grade or mark?

Where profiles of competencies or skills contribute to formal assessment they have to produce a single mark, grade or pass/fail decision. It is not easy to see how this can be done without undermining the whole rationale of profiles as representing a multi-dimensional picture of an individual. It can lead to rating scales being turned into mark scales and added up, producing very curious results, or a global mark being awarded on the basis of an impressionistic overview of a profile, introducing unacceptable subjectivity and unreliability.

Is profiling a 'one-off' activity or part of an ongoing process?

Profiling doesn't make much sense as a one-off activity used to assess a single assignment or even as an assessment method on an individual module. It arguably works best over an extended period of time during which there is ample opportunity for students to use a profile to set learning goals, to pick up skills in different ways as opportunities arise in order to fill gaps, and to review and summarise progress. Profiling systems currently in use extend for up to four years. They often operate alongside modules, spanning learning across a range of topics and experiences, rather than as part of a regularly timetabled and tightly-focussed module. This can mean that profiling falls into the background of students' concerns with their current modules in the foreground to such an extent that they forget all about it until the next profiling meeting comes round, rather than using profiles as a constant background to their learning.

Who will be involved?

As with most student centred assessment methods there is a range of possible student involvement. Most commonly competency profiles are tutor-specified and tutor-marked with students responsible for providing evidence for tutors to judge against the profile. Sometimes students self-assess prior to a viva with a tutor who makes the final assessment decisions. In work-based contexts supervisors may also assess, sometimes prior to self assessment, sometimes as part of a three-way assessment with student, tutor and supervisor gradings contributing equally. It is unusual for students to design their own profiles.

As profiling often spans quite long periods of study it is necessary that the tutor involved knows the student and is aware of changes over time in the student's development and competence. This may mean that the student's personal tutor becomes involved because no-one else follows the student through their entire course, especially on modular courses. This may place a heavy burden on a role which has almost disappeared in many institutions: many personal tutors have too little contact with their tutees to be able to make any judgments about them. It may also compromise the non-judgmental counselling role personal tutors perform.

How are learning outcomes described?
Profiling systems often have very vague descriptions of the competencies or skills they include, sometimes amounting to little more than a label such as 'interpersonal skills'. For assessment purposes this is inadequate. To orient students, to produce reliable and fair judgments and to improve consistency of marking between tutors, learning outcomes need to be properly specified. A number of institutions have introduced the compulsory specification of learning outcomes in module descriptions but few have adequately trained lecturers how to write outcome statements in forms which are sufficiently robust to support assessment, though there are exceptions. Walker (1994) explains the rationale for outcomes, provides guidelines and examples from many different types of courses, written in different forms, and links lists of outcome statements to the use of profiling.

What evidence is required of competence?
Industry uses assessment centres if it wants to reliably distinguish applicants' skills, so that behaviour can be observed directly. In contrast, higher education largely relies on documentary evidence or written self-reporting which will probably be less reliable and may not be capable of assessing the skill at all. Where forms of evidence can be negotiated it can be difficult to interpret archived documents, testimonials or peer feedback. Specifying appropriate forms of evidence is as important as specifying criteria. Often a single piece of evidence contributes to several competencies, and judgments about each competency are influenced by several pieces of evidence. This is different from tutors' normal experiences of marking single pieces of work against a single global criterion of quality, and is much more difficult.

What criteria and standards are used to judge the evidence?
Even quite detailed profiles can leave markers completely adrift when it comes to deciding if a student is competent or not and can leave students confused about whether they are competent or what they would need to be able to be assessed as competent. The whole NVQ movement has been dogged

by reports of wide variations in marking standards even with the much higher levels of specification of more detailed competencies than is normally the case in higher education.

Where negotiation is involved, as with using profiles to frame project work, students may gain a clearer understanding at the outset of what would count as an acceptable outcome.

What formative documentation is involved?

If profiling is to be an ongoing process then the documentation should encourage and allow frequent use, and reveal development and change over time. The way profiles are written makes a great deal of difference from how students use them. Questions, exercises and materials which encourage formative self assessment and reflection can be useful, though they are likely to require face-to-face contact and discussion if they are to be taken seriously. If rating scales are used it can be useful to leave space for self assessment as well as tutor judgments at several stages in students' development, and room for comments and advice about progress.

What final documentation is involved?

With 'portfolio' type profiles, if there is no specification of the final form the profile should take, then there should at least be guidance or models available. If some forms of documentation are unacceptable (and there are always limits, even with open-ended schemes) this should be made clear.

Profiles which identify competencies or the achievement of learning outcomes in a summative form need to be easily interpretable by those for whom they are produced who may not understand the way the course or profiling works.

Case Studies

Profiling subject-related knowledge and skills in English Studies

Alan Jenkins, Educational Methods Unit, Oxford Brookes University

Innovator: Rob Pope, English Studies, Oxford Brookes University

Course Context

Profiling of subject related knowledge and skills has been developed as one aspect of a major reorientation of English Studies at Oxford Brookes University (in the Modular Course at this institution). English was previously conceived as English literature, and taught and assessed in a conventional teacher-centred manner, emphasising unseen examinations and teacher-assessed essays. The revised course considers a wider range of texts, and more emphasis is placed on the students' interpretation of and rewriting of texts. Assessment has been radically changed to:

- assess certain defined critical, creative and communicative skills, e.g. working in groups, information handling;

- identify the key knowledge and skills that can be developed through English Studies, e.g. textual analysis, redrafting, text production;

- assess a wider variety of processes and products, i.e. types of writing and speaking modes of composition;

- involve and empower students by giving them a greater role in their own assessment;

- enable and require students to profile their developing competencies in terms of the knowledge and skills they have developed through their English Studies.

This has involved full-time staff agreeing common procedures for the 140–170 students who take the compulsory modules in year 1 and the 90–100 students who specialise in English Studies in each of years 2 and 3. These changes have been planned over three to four years, and are in the process of full implementation. The emphasis on profiling is seen as a key element of student self assessment. The development of profiling was also an opportunistic strategy to enable the group to bid for funds from the Enterprise Unit, which is charged with implementing profiling for all students. The actual form and procedures as to how profiling is to take place is currently an issue for debate within the institution. English Studies is arguing that profiling should focus on the knowledge and skills that are developed through disciplines. It is sceptical of – even hostile to – an emphasis (such as in BTEC courses) on a profiling system that would emphasise common and core skills. It fears that such an emphasis would give undue prominence to training at the expense of education, while profiling based in disciplines will better engage all staff and students.

Description of Assessment

As part of the course's revision, much initial discussion centred on defining the core knowledge and skills that staff (and student representatives) considered most important and appropriate to a course in English Studies. All modules are now required to clearly identify knowledge and skills and to ensure that the assessment system enables students to develop these skills. Some modules are required to include a minimum of 20% of marks to students' self-assessment. This description now focuses on the subject profile.

This takes the form of a statement of around 500 words written by the student. These statements are required at two stages of the course:

- at the end of year 1, after the student has completed the three compulsory modules of year 1 (a module represents around one ninth/tenth of a full-time student's work in an academic year);

- at the end of the compulsory synoptic double module taken in the last two terms of year 3.

Feeding into the profile is the student's 'Course Journal'. Many of the core/compulsory modules require students to keep an academic journal. Much of this remains private to the students. They are encouraged each week to write an entry that (a) looks back to what they wrote/planned in the previous week, and (b) reflects on what they have learnt through participation in the reading and classroom sessions during this week, and to look forward as to how they can build in this week's experience. As the example of the 'Weekly Study and Learning Pattern' shows (see Appendix B), this involves students in reflection and self-assessment and in profiling their development through the course. It represents – should students do it – a considerable emphasis on students' formative self-assessment.

When challenged as to whether students will fully participate if these activities remain essentially private, the central response of staff is that if the modules are effectively taught then the journal will be so central to students' learning that the student will see its value and the early evidence is that this is so. However, a further inducement for students to take this reflection seriously is that some of the assessments for modules will require them to choose and use some of the private writings for course assignments.

The central profile statements will be 500 word statements written by students to brief guidelines devised by staff (see guidelines Appendix A, p.131). These will be compulsory requirements for their courses. The course regulations clearly state that the student who does not hand in the profile statement will not pass that module and will thus fail his/her degree. The profile statement will not, however, be graded.

Evaluation

The staff's philosophy is that there is no one way to write text. Accordingly they consider that students should have considerable freedom on how to write their profile statements. Each statement will be a statement of what one individual considers she/he has learnt through the discipline. To grade that statement would accordingly devalue what students consider they had achieved. It remains to be seen whether the necessity to produce the profile and the close relationship between it and the way the course is taught will be sufficient inducement for students to put effort into the task.

Initial feedback and course evaluation after the first year of operation confirm that the 'journal' is generally typed up and the end of course 'summary profiling' is found largely valuable. This part of the redesign, at any rate, appears to be a great success. The regular weekly (personal) review that finally feeds into the 'Summary Profile' is harder to trace and gauge, but most students do seem to be doing it, perhaps because it feeds into seminars directly.

Discussion

A subject profile – which is clearly linked to a weekly reflective journal entry – seems potentially an effective device for helping students to articulate for themselves what they are learning throughout their subject studies. Depending on the way the subject is taught, and the guidance given to students, subject-based profiles can help students to integrate transferable skills into their everyday academic practice. They offer a powerful way to direct the student to give themselves formative assessment and to make periodic summative assessment of their learning.

Clearly it is particularly appropriate to an English Studies course, where the analysis, production and rewriting of texts is central to the practice of the course. However, its basic ideas could be adapted to the teaching of any discipline.

Careful evaluation of the course is required to ensure that the profile statements are taken seriously by students. In certain cases this might mean that they should be graded.

Appendix A

SUMMARY PROFILES: ENGLISH STUDIES

At the end of your English Studies Stage I (module 2306) and Stage II (module 2392), you are required to put together two 500-word summaries of your experience of, respectively, part of and all of your English course at Oxford Brookes University. This will be based in large measure on your 'Course Journals' for these two modules and guided by the general criteria proposed in the English Studies Handbook (section 3.2) and the course books for modules 2306 and 2392.

What follows, therefore, is really no more than a reminder of the kinds of issue you should address in your summary profiles. Their precise formulation, articulation and mode of presentation is up to you.

Issues such as:

- the kind of KNOWLEDGE(S) you have developed (textual, critical, historical, theoretical, etc.);

- the direct relevance – or otherwise – of these knowledges to (1) your immediate personal and social situation, your present needs and desires, and (2) your longer-term life and career goals;

- the kind of skills you have developed (personal and interpersonal, oral and written, individual and collective; research; presentational; word-processing, etc.);

- the direct applicability – or otherwise – of these skills to (1) your immediate personal situation and social context, your present needs and desires; (2) your longer term life and career goals;

- where, in as general or as specific terms as you wish, do you see yourself 'coming from' and 'going to' via the English Studies part of the programme?

All these knowledges and skills, and many more specific ones not mentioned here, will have formed the core of your work in English Studies. They are explored and developed in various degrees and configurations throughout your modules. They are also the subject of specific focusing and re-focusing in modules 2306 and 2392.

However, the most immediate and important 'subject' engaged in this educational process is you. It is therefore most immediately and importantly up to you to give the only profile of this course that ultimately matters: your own.

Appendix B

Profiling in English Studies: continuing processes and final products

Here are some guidelines on how you can build up your own 'profile', week by week and at the end of your first and final years. These guidelines are therefore of especial relevance to: 'Texts, Problems and Approaches' (2306, Stage I, terms 2 and 3) and 'Critical Issues and Strategies: English Studies Synoptic' (2392, Stage II, final year, terms 2 and 3). The principles, however, apply to all your English Studies modules.

WEEKLY STUDY AND LEARNING PATTERN

1 Preparation

Have I read over last week's study sheet, in particular noting the two things I promised myself to do this week? What were they?

Summary of the reading, research, exercises, writing and planning I have done before this week's group session (50 words max.):

Two issues, pieces of information, texts or strategies I shall contribute to a seminar agenda:

2 Participation

Generally: In what ways have I contributed to the shaping of the group agenda?

   And in what ways have my attitudes and knowledge been shaped or refined by that agenda?

Particularly: In what ways and how far am I doing the following too little or too much, on or off the point:

   - speaking?
   - listening?
   - working on my own?
   - working with others?

3 Retrospect

Looking back over both my preparation and participation for this week's session(s), What kinds of new knowledge did I acquire, extend or refine to do with English Studies?

What study techniques, technical strategies and theoretical models did I use? (And which techniques, strategies and models might I have used but didn't?)

In what ways did I make positive efforts to improve my skills in speaking? listening? working on my own? working with others?

What two things do I promise myself to do next week so as to learn from and build upon this week's experience? (Are these the same as or different from last week's promises?)

Profiling BTEC common skills in Civil Engineering

Alan Jenkins, Educational Methods Unit, Oxford Brookes University

Innovator: Nick Spencer Chapman, Civil Engineering and
Building Division, Oxford Brookes University

Course Context

This is a three-year full-time course, with around 20 students per year. The second year is spent on full-time work experience. The students will graduate with a Higher National Diploma in Civil Engineering Studies. The students on the course mainly have one A-level, usually of a low grade, or come from a BTEC National Diploma or Certificate background. There are also usually one or two mature students with experience in the construction industry. The first year HND civil engineering students differ from their peers on the degree course mainly in terms of failure to organise themselves, to submit work on time and to demonstrate various other 'common skills' (see below). Typically about half the students qualifying with an HND go onto the Division's degree course where, perhaps surprisingly, they tend to excel.

It seems that their failure to qualify for a degree course at age 18 results from inadequate common skills rather than from any innate lack of ability. It is also possible that the interest inspired by vocational work stimulates the development of personal skills.

This course is highly determined by outside professional requirements. It has to meet the requirements of the Engineering Council and in particular the requirements of the Business and Technology Education Council (BTEC). They set out very explicit requirements concerning course delivery. These include the requirements that the following common skills are developed and assessed.

Though students have no say in determining these skills, they are required to be involved in providing evidence of achieving and assessing them through self assessment and negotiated assessment with tutors and workplace supervisors. Students are required to keep track of their own skills development through a profile and identify, with their tutors, areas for remedial action. For students to pass the course they have to obtain a pass grade in all the common skills. On qualification they are issued by BTEC with a 'Notification of Performance' stating the grade they have obtained in each of the common skills.

Assessment

An introductory skills module in term 1 of year 1 emphasises the importance of skill development in the course and in students' future professional roles. It also gives students training and experience in self and peer assessment and explains the procedures for the assessment of core skills. Students are

---

COMMON SKILLS AND OUTCOMES

Common skill		Outcome
A Managing and developing self	1.	Manage own roles and responsibilities
	2.	Manage own time in achieving objectives
	3.	Undertakes personal and career development
	4.	Transfer skills gained to new and changing situations and contexts
B Working with and relating to others	5.	Treat others' values, beliefs and opinions with respect
	6.	Relate to and interact effectively with individuals and groups
	7.	Work effectively as a member of a team
C Communicating	8.	Receive and respond to a variety of information
	9.	Present information in a variety of visual forms
	10.	Communicating in writing
	11.	Participate in oral and non-verbal communication
D Managing tasks and solving problems	12.	Use information sources
	13.	Deal with a combination of routine and non-routine tasks
	14.	Identify and solve routine and non-routine problems
E Applying numerary	15.	Apply numerical skills and techniques
F Applying technology	16.	Use a range of technological equipment and systems
G Applying design and creativity	17.	Apply a range of skills and techniques to develop a variety of ideas in the creation of new/modified products, services or situations
	18.	Use a range of thought processes.

allocated an individual personal tutor for the duration of the course. Each personal tutor has three students on this course per year, and nine students over the three years of the course.

Throughout the course students are required to keep a logbook in which they record their own assessment of common skills outcomes and present supporting evidence. Each year the student will have around three meetings with the personal tutor. The first will be mainly focused on helping the student to identify their existing competencies and those which need to be developed. In subsequent meetings the student will present evidence of accomplishment concerning certain specific skills or competencies and will state the grade she/he considers she/he should receive. The student can present any evidence she/he considers relevant, including tutor-marked work or activities from outside the course (e.g. Students' Union or sporting achievements). Evidence from the industrial training period is regarded as particularly important in the final year. The grade allocated is negotiated between the student and her/his personal tutor.

At the end, student and tutor will agree a grade for all the common skills. However, the final grade for the common skills will be decided by a staff examination committee, using the evidence of the student profile and logbook. It has been agreed that the grades awarded will reflect the final level of competence demonstrated. Poor initial competencies should therefore not prejudice the final grade.

Evaluation

This is the first year of the innovation so any evaluation has to be tentative. Many students initially found the idea of common skills irrelevant to studies of engineering, and were surprised at the requirement for self-assessment. Some staff were worried whether students would take it seriously, and questioned whether students had the knowledge/skills to assess themselves. Staff have also been doubtful of their own competence in that area and uncertain as to how common skills interviews should proceed. To an extent, these problems are disappearing as students and staff gain experience. It will be interesting to see whether the year in industry helps students to identify the skills they need to develop, and indeed assists in skills development.

However, students and staff are now concerned about the subjectivity of the grading of the common skills. They consider that much depends upon the skill of the student in arguing their case (a common skill in its own right, of course), and that there is a general problem about interpreting criteria for students and personal tutors. Attempts to clarify criteria with further explanatory documents is seen as making the paperwork more cumbersome and less likely to be consulted.

Discussion

As staff and students gain experience of the new system, they are starting to identify possible development to improve present practice. These include:

- clearer and fuller assessment criteria;

- clearer targeting of modes of study and coursework assessment tasks to specific skills;

- more discussion between tutors concerning assessment criteria and the conduct of assessment interviews;

- targeting of certain skills in specific modules rather than trying to assess all skills in all modules.

Profiling the trainee teacher

Alan Jenkins, Educational Methods Unit, Oxford Brookes University

Innovator: Robin McClelland, School of Education,
Oxford Brookes University

Course Context

A four-year full-time course for trainee teachers is part of the University's large modular degree structure and there is also a longer part-time route. There are 15 full-time tutors on the course, 90–95 students in year 1 and 85 students in year 2 with similar numbers expected in years 3 and 4 as the cohorts move through.

As a central feature of a major course review, the School of Education introduced a system in which students profile their own progress through the course and keep a formative record of their development. In the previous course, students were not required or encouraged to keep any record of assessment of their own academic or professional development. There were judgments of students made by staff, and these were confidential to the staff. This teacher-dominated assessment, and a system which put little responsibility onto the students, was considered inappropriate for students who were adults. Moreover, most of them would enter a teaching profession which was moving to the view of the teacher as someone who continually reviews and develops his or her own professional knowledge and skills. In addition, they would be teaching pupils who were increasingly being required to assess themselves and develop their own record of achievement. Given students' future career development, it was decided that their own education should prepare them for taking responsibility for their own professional development and helping their pupils to reflect on their own development.

Students take a variety of college-based modules on aspects of education and classroom practice, and in years 3 and 4 there are also extensive periods of school-based practice.

Description of the Assessment

As part of the fundamental review of the course, staff agreed a set of seven criteria for professional development which embody the necessary skills for the classroom practitioner (see 'Profile 2' p138). All modules had to be written so as to clearly state professional areas they should develop, to make clear the specific learning objectives the student should achieve and how the assessment of the module was designed to help the students develop those skills.

Amongst staff this led to a greater collegiate sense of what they were trying to achieve and students now know more clearly what is expected of them. This, however, remained a teacher defined and dominated area of the curriculum. During the review, staff discussed the possibility of students helping to define module objectives, but decided that this was not compatible with operating at higher SSRs.

For each education module students take they complete a 'Profile 1' (see below). At the beginning of the module they write down the assessment criteria after they have been explained and discussed in class. As they hand in coursework they will be asked to evaluate their work against these criteria. The staff decided not to get students to assess themselves in the sense of suggesting a grade as they feared this would focus the student on the grade rather than the formative evaluation of their professional development.

The tutors then make their assessment and grade the work in the light of the student's statement. When students receive the tutor's comments they are urged in the light of their own and the tutor's comments to set personal development targets. This happens on every education module.

All students are allocated a personal tutor. Once a year the student and tutor meet for a one-to-one discussion of the student's sense of their progress in developing professional competencies. Students are urged to re-read all 'Profile 1' forms and to bring them to the tutorial. They are required to have started to fill in 'Profile 2'. Students and their tutors then discuss progress and target areas for future development. Students write their view of these and an action plan explaining how they will achieve them. This 'Profile 2' form is then signed by tutor and student and a copy is kept by both.

A 'Profile 3' form is now being developed for school experience. This, again, will be initially completed by the student and then discussed and agreed with the school experience tutor (who is unlikely to be the personal tutor) and the person responsible for helping and monitoring the student in school. There will be three copies of this form: one to be held by the student, one by the University and one by the school.

Evaluation

The informal evidence is that staff and students are very positive about the introduction of profiling. Staff and students say that objectives and clear assessment criteria provide clearer guidance for students concerning what is expected of them; students get clearer and more consistent messages from their different education modules; students and tutors comment that the meetings to discuss 'Profile 2' forms benefit from the student's formative evaluations on 'Profile 1' forms; the meetings themselves are described as purposeful and positive; students appear (to staff) as more in control and clearer about their learning goals and professional development than their predecessors. Staff are positive about their role as profiling tutors and compare it to the previous vague role of the personal tutor and the frequent difficulty they subsequently had of writing references for past personal tutees they hardly knew. Using the system of 'Profile 1' and 'Profile 2' forms, is

---

Profile 1

Module Title and Number

Student:

Copies to:　　Student ....

　　　　　　　Seminar Tutor .... Personal Tutor..

Module Assignment

Criteria Statements by which assignment will be assessed

Student evaluation using these statements

Tutor Evaluation and grading using these statements

Student set targets

---

simple to understand and administrate. The School is not saddled with holding and organising masses of paper, yet does develop a good record of the students' development. Some students seem to be more successful than others in taking control: these are often the mature students.

Due to resource problems the staff are now considering grouping students for profiling conversations and helping students to initially profile each other before discussion with the tutor.

Profile 2
Review of Term .... Year ....
Discussion document to be used with Tutor

Student ....
Personal tutor...

Profile Criteria

1. Personal and professional relationships
2. Understanding the learning process
3. Structuring the learning experience
4. Understanding, organising and managing the learning environment
5. Assessment, evaluation and reflection
6. Personal and professional attributes
7. Specialist subject expertise

How I see my progress this term:

Bibliography

Assiter, A. and E. Shaw, eds, (1993), *Using Records of Achievement in Higher Education*. London: Kogan Page

Broadfoot, T. P. ed, (1986), *Profiles and Records of Achievement: A Review of Issues and Practice*, Holt, Rinehart and Winston

Broadfoot, T. P. (1988), *Introducing Profiling*, London: MacMillan

BTEC (1991), *Common Skills: General Guideline*, BTEC

Evans, M. (1988), *Practical Profiling*, London: Routledge and Kegan Paul

Fenwick, A., A. Assiter and N. Nixon, (1992), *Profiling in Higher Education*, Department of Employment: HMSO

Fenwick, A. and N. Nixon, (1992), *Profiling Work-based Learning in Academic Courses*. London: CNAA

Gillham, B. (1993), *Profiling*, Red Guides Series 2, No 2, Northumbria University

Hitchcock, G. (1990), *Profiles and Profiling: A Practical Introduction*, Longman

Law, B. (1984), *Uses and abuses of profiling: a handbook of reviewing and recording students' experience and achievement*, London: Harper and Row

Nuttal, D. and H. Goldstein, (1984), 'Profiles and Graded Tests: the Technical Issues', in Further Education Unit, *Profiles in Action*

Otter, S. (1989), *Competence* , Leicester University: UDACE

Pope, R. (1994), 'A Very English Profile? A Model for subject-based development and an argument for peculiar practices in profiling', in A. Jenkins and L. Walker, eds, *Developing Student Capability through Modular Courses*, London: Kogan Page

Walker, L. (1994), *Guidance for Writing Learning Outcomes*, Oxford: Oxford Brookes University

9 Using Portfolios

Introduction

Portfolios have in the past been most widely used in creative subjects such as art and design where students collect their best artwork together in a large folder. The use of various forms of portfolio is spreading to subject areas as varied as Engineering and English and, inevitably, becoming more varied in form and purpose. Portfolios are used to:

- judge a wide range of products of students' work together, in order to gain a rounded overview of achievement over a period of time rather than a narrow sample at one moment in time;

- assess process as well as outcome in learning, by including evidence of learning and achievement at several stages of development;

- provide a flexible vehicle through which a students' development and direction can be plotted, reviewed and reflected upon in order to guide future learning, emphasising that no learning is ever complete;

- ensure that students engage in a wide variety of learning activities rather than being selective or leaving everything until revision time, while minimising the marking load associated with frequent assessment;

- provide a vehicle for collating evidence, from past experience or work experience, that competencies have been achieved;

- provide documentary evidence of ability and experience for students to show employers or clients.

As with diaries and logs there is a real tension between the formative role of supporting learning which might involve portfolios containing the most revealing of students' work, failures, blind allies and all, and their summative role which could involve presenting carefully selected work to put the best possible gloss on achievements – as with an art students' final exhibition. And as with diaries and logs, these two forms are often best kept separate.

Practical matters

Portfolios as collections of finished assignments

In Engineering a portfolio might contain all the lab reports, problem sheets and exercises undertaken during a laboratory course. It might be marked for completeness, to ensure that students attend and write up all the labs, with selected reports assessed for different goals, such as communication skills or accuracy, but without all the contents of the portfolio being assessed for every goal. In this way students have to pay attention to every aspect of the course but marking is kept to a minimum. This succeeds in maintaining the level of learning activity but is not student centred in any other respect unless there are opportunities for, for example, formative peer assessment or sharing between students at various stages during the course. It is also possible to engage students in various group activities but require the submission of an individual portfolio as evidence of individual engagement with every aspect of the group assignments.

Portfolios as collections of best work

In a creative subject this might involve the best design studies, in Music, audio tapes of the best musical performances. In Social Science students could be asked to collect not only their three best essays but also their three best seminar presentations, three best book reviews and their best piece of survey research, into a portfolio. In Science a portfolio might contain the four best lab reports, the five best problem sheets and the best project. This can free formative assessment of coursework from the need to allocate marks and allow formative feedback, including peer assessment, to improve work, encouraging students to use this feedback instead of ignoring it. It is helpful to specify the types of work required and vital to specify criteria for assessment. It may also be necessary to make completion of coursework tasks compulsory, even if those not eventually included in the portfolio are not marked.

Portfolios as profiles of the student, for employers

Art students' portfolios are used in job interviews, and, having interviewed such students for graphic design jobs, I can vouch for the revealing nature of such portfolios compared with other kinds of assessment evidence. In a less product-oriented subject or where products (such as essays) are not easy to review quickly such portfolios resemble 'Records of Achievement' (see chapter 8, Using Profiles) and can contain a wide variety of documentary evidence, including testimonials, certificates, examples of work or self reviews.

Portfolios as vehicles for reflection on learning

Portfolios may resemble logs, recording all learning activities undertaken and all the products of that activity: notes on reading, calculations, drawings, reports, handouts, newspaper cuttings, photocopies of extracts from articles and so on, rather like a scrapbook, making a comprehensive record of the student's learning on the course. Students usually have something resembling such a portfolio already, though they may exclude anything other than lecture notes and handouts, not considering films they have seen, visits they have been on or chats they have had as valid contributions to their learning and they may not know how to file less easily categorisable material.

Such a portfolio may not either lead to additional learning or provide a basis for assessment unless there is also evidence of reflection and of what students have done with all the material. An Education course which used such a reflective portfolio in assessment used the criterion of 'evidence of quality of engagement with the material' and explained what was meant by it and this prompted much written reflection as students attempted to capture and record learning points and experiences.

Portfolios as evidence of process

When Architecture students present finished designs for assessment they often also present a portfolio of draft and rejected designs, revealing the way the end design was arrived at and the kinds of thinking which went on. This can be enormously revealing. Similarly, with design tasks or problems in Engineering, portfolios can be used to reveal the way the problem was analysed and the way alternative solutions were considered and developed before the final solution was adopted and implemented. Conventional project reports or finished designs hide all this evidence about process – usually deliberately. It is common to use a viva based around such a portfolio to moderate marks awarded for the finished product or to allocate a proportion of marks for evidence of the quality of the design process or problem solving process. Similarly, it would be possible to use portfolios of writing and reading to reveal how dissertations or extended essays were arrived at and to award marks for the research and writing process.

Portfolios as evidence of achievement of competencies or standards

The system for obtaining professional recognition in educational development in the UK does not involve an exam and there are no formal courses or qualifications available. Instead it involves preparing a portfolio of evidence that a specified range of experiences (such as running workshops or assessing staff development needs) has been undertaken so as to demonstrate a specified range of values (for example, underpinning practice with research or concern for equal opportunities). Such portfolios take a considerable period of time to prepare, both in terms of obtaining the appropriate experiences and in terms of documenting them in appropriate ways. The final portfolios can reach two 200-page volumes, mostly containing evidence such as workshop programmes and feedback, letters, reports and so on, carefully organised and commented on to explain how the evidence meets all the formal requirements. This is very similar to using profiles for accrediting prior learning (see chapter 8, Using Profiles) but with a central emphasis on the collation of a portfolio of evidence which will meet all assessment requirements in one go. Such portfolios almost always require the use of a viva after assessors have familiarised themselves with the documentary evidence and often require the use of two assessors in order to cope with the variety of forms of evidence they are confronted with in a consistent way. As with a PhD viva, an applicant can usually pass, fail or be referred with specific requirements to meet before a pass decision can be made.

Key Issues

What form should portfolios take?

Because the purpose of using portfolios is not always thought through, what they should contain is not always specified, and tutors end up with huge piles of uninterpretable material and students end up thoroughly confused and exhausted. The types of use specified in above each lead to very different contents. Students should be given a clear rationale, a clear specification of the kinds of contents they should be collecting. It is unhelpful to a student who has never used portfolios before to say they they can put in it whatever they like. Maximum and minimum sizes should be specified as there will always be a trade off between quantity and quality and limits to what a tutor can review. As with many forms of assessment of student centred courses it is important to employ a facilitative degree of structure and with portfolios this may initially be a considerable degree of structure.

As well as understanding why the portfolio is being put together and the kinds of things it should contain, students need to know whether the material in it should be expected to 'speak for itself' or whether a commentary or reflective note is required. If a viva is not being used in assessment such a commentary may be vital.

Portfolios also need to be well organised, with a clear contents list and possibly a system for cross referencing. Where portfolios present material against an extended set of requirements for evidence of experience and competence or values, careful organisation is vital and distinguishes the quality of candidates almost as much as does the content.

How do tutors cope with the variety and volume of material?

Tutors need a clear statement of purpose which guides specification of content, and clear criteria which can accommodate different kinds of material; without them assessment becomes extremely difficult. Tutors also need standards, for example, what would count as an adequate amount of experience or an acceptable lab report or sufficient evidence of reflection? The volume of material is a secondary question because it may not all need to be read with great care or even read at all, as portfolios may be sampled in order to gain an impression of the way students go about their studies, rather than checking off every single item of content. That a lab report is present may only take a moment to confirm. That it meets particular criteria will take longer, but how long will depend on the criteria. The use of portfolios for a practical-based Engineering course at the University of Hertfordshire reduced assessment time to 25% of the previous load by only assessing one of the many lab reports in the portfolio against each of the criteria (though the students could not know which one) instead of assessing them all against every criteria. Allowing video-tapes will take huge amounts of assessment time. Allowing photographs or other unconventional material may make criteria difficult to apply. If it is intended that students should be able to put anything in they like then it may be necessary to abandon the intention to produce a mark. And, of course, portfolios used primarily to encourage reflection may not require a tutor's response at all.

What criteria are used to assess portfolios?

It is easier to specify what kinds of material should go into a portfolio than it is to specify whether what students put in them is acceptable or up to standard. Distinguishing standards for first-year and third-year portfolios is even harder than it is for essays and producing anything beyond pass/fail decisions may be impossible without an extremely thorough specification of learning outcomes, criteria and standards. If several tutors are involved, marking guidelines and calibration exercises may be necessary.

Does the use of a portfolio result in the desired and appropriate kind of learning activity ?

If portfolios are used to increase reflection, does this actually happen and how would you know? If it is designed to focus students' attention on key competencies and to seek learning opportunities and evidence, does this happen, and how would you know? If it is designed to maintain a wide range of learning activity does this happen or do students do nothing at all except what they can record in their portfolio? Portfolios are capable of corrupting learning as well as supporting it, leading to unproductive busywork and the collection of quantities of meaningless resources instead of quality of engagement. Students can learn to fake almost anything, including 'quality of engagement with the course' or 'reflection on learning' and can become extrinsically motivated in their collection of material, painting a distorted picture of the way they are learning. They will tend to do this when the wrong assessment criteria are used or when it is appropriate only to comment on portfolios rather than to mark them. Gaining students' commitment will depend on their understanding what portfolios are for, believing this and knowing how to make portfolios work for them.

Are students trained to collect and build portfolios? Do they have 'models' to emulate?

For most students portfolios will be entirely new and they will need clear guidance on how to use them. The distinction between presenting a 'best case' and reflecting in ways which support learning is particularly difficult to get to grips with. Early on students need to see examples of complete portfolios – good, bad and indifferent – and to understand why they are good or bad. They need examples of the kinds of materials they could collate. They may benefit from a limited range to start with and with specific requirements for pieces of reflection in order to get going. And they need to discuss the process of starting portfolios with their peers.

Should portfolios be collated at the time of assessment or throughout learning?

Although the use of portfolios for summative assessment of prior learning can take place after most of the learning has finished, most other forms must be used over time as an integral part of learning and contributing to the learning. This means that students should have the time, support and encouragement to make regular entries and additions. At several stages during the collation of their portfolios, it may also be helpful to students to have some tutor feedback, or at least some peer feedback from other students who are also collating portfolios. Students need to see how others do it and how others are getting on and how much is being included, to get new ideas for kinds of materials which can be used and ways in which they can be used. As time goes on they need to become more selective and organised, discarding some contents, writing reflective notes and seeking other contents.

Case Studies

The use of portfolios in assessment of an Archaeology course

Jessica Claridge, Staff Development, University of Exeter

Innovator: Linda Hurcombe, Department of History and Archaeology, University of Exeter

Course Context
'Archaeological Theory and Practice I' is a second year course for single honours Archaeologists, designed to put into practice some of the theoretical concepts introduced in a 'Principles and Methods' course that all students of Archaeology take in year 1. It consists largely of practical classes concerning surveying, computing, and environmental archaeology (pollen and bones). Most other modules are conventionally taught – with lectures, seminars, tutorials and practical classes – and conventionally assessed via essays, practical reports and exams, with a dissertation in the final year.

Assessment
The assessment involves two assignments and a portfolio of practical work containing maps, plans artifact drawings, photographs and the like. Details of how the portfolio should be tackled, with criteria for presentation and assessment and deadlines are given on a written sheet at the beginning of the course. The group is small and much discussion takes place between staff and students.

There is formal session each week on a different area to develop students' critical faculties with relation to their portfolios, e.g. location maps. Students are guided and constantly supervised. One member of staff has likened the process to an apprenticeship. Apart from the formal sessions it is open house and students may constantly question staff in the drawing office. Students are expected to establish their own rules about how and what they do. By the end of the course it is hoped that they will have developed their own set of values for interpreting evidence.

The portfolio has three areas:

1.	Computing

2.	Pollen/bones

These are both dealt with in depth during Terms 1 and 2 and each has a set assignment.

3.	Archaeological illustration. This has to include:

- map – location or distribution;
- diagram – produced from primary material;
- artifact drawing – pottery, metalwork, organise material and stone plus an optional area;
- site photography.

Criteria

Students may expand on any of the areas involved if they wish and develop mini-projects within the portfolio. This would be considered 'value-added' for assessment purposes but students have got to explain the theme.

The standard of presentation is taken into account for assessment: material in the Archaeological Illustration section should be of 'publication standard', as for an archaeological journal, and submitted in mounted form.

Students have to show that an illustration works: that it is comprehensible and fulfils the right criteria. Students need to be able to show that they understand the professional conventions of the way things are done.

It is made clear that it is quality that counts, not quantity. The overall physical size of the portfolio is specified.

There has to be a list of contents.

All illustrations must be fully captioned with courses.

If computer graphics are used, the software must be indicated.

Late submission is given a 'fail' mark unless there are extenuating circumstances when an 'ill' mark can be returned.

Students are expected to be able to use desk-top publishing packages. As the quality of this output is not considered high enough for archaeological journals in certain aspects, they also have to be able to re-draw anything they need 'to publication standard'.

Evaluation

The building of the second-year portfolio helps students to prepare for the dissertation they have to do in year 3, which is expected to have the 'publication standard' illustration as well as scholarly content. It helps students learn to collate and present information coherently. Students all reach a high standard of production and acquire skills during the course which must be of benefit to them whatever field they choose to move into.

Both staff and students are very committed to the work that is involved in the 'all round' learning that takes place while the portfolio is being put together. The course and the building of the portfolio is given a lot of time by the members of staff involved, both during the course and for the assessment.

The portfolios are assessed by all staff involved in the course: four lecturers and two specialist archaeological technicians. They are looking for how far the portfolios satisfy the different elements the students have been asked to include and how far beyond this they have gone. All students do well, some very well.

Modularisation and the timetable changes which have accompanied this have rushed both the production and assessment of the portfolio which requires an extended period of time.

Portfolios for assessment in Education

Liz McDowell, University of Northumbria

Innovator: Colin Biott and the Course Team of the Postgraduate Diploma/MEd in Educational Development, University of Northumbria at Newcastle

Course Context

The Postgraduate Diploma/MEd in Educational Development is a part-time, evening-only course for teachers and trainers. It is a modular course, and students undertake two core modules and three option modules. After this they either complete a project for the award of a Postgraduate Diploma or complete an additional double core module and a dissertation for the award of MEd. Each module lasts for ten weeks with a scheduled class contact of three hours per week.

The course is highly student centred. Teachers of all age ranges and trainers from a wide variety of contexts are accepted onto the course, which is concerned with generic issues relevant to all education contexts. It is the student's responsibility to contextualise these general themes and ensure that the course is relevant and useful to their own professional practice. Students are encouraged to pursue their own interests and there is a high degree of negotiation of module content between tutors and the student group.

Assessment

Students are required to submit a portfolio after the completion of each option module. Portfolios must contain a negotiated selection from the following: case study materials; a literature review or annotated bibliography; a summary and discussion of themes and issues from the literature and from the student's own professional experience; a reflective professional diary; reports on elements of the course including individual or group present-ation/seminars; indexed fieldwork data.

The portfolios provide a focus for discussion and formative feedback between students and tutors. Students determine the extent to which they attempt to analyse, reflect critically or synthesise ideas at the time at which they complete a module. Students also choose the form of the portfolio bearing in mind the need to initiate helpful dialogue with their tutor. Students propose the criteria by which they wish their portfolio to be judged and submit a criteria and comments sheet.

In addition to their use for formative feedback and discussion, the portfolios build cumulatively towards the completion of a composite assignment after all three option modules have been completed. This assignment requires students to reflect on the themes and issues emerging from the course in relation to their own learning. Material from at least two of their options must be used and the portfolios are vital resources for the completion of the assignment.

Evaluation

Portfolios were introduced when the course changed to a modular structure. The approach was chosen as an alternative to separately assessing each module in order to avoid fragmentation and an over-emphasis on assessment and also to ensure a reasonable workload for part-time students. It is intended that the preparation of portfolios is a worthwhile process in itself, not something done as an obligation after the learning has taken place.

Most students have appreciated the portfolio approach and have produced work of an acceptable standard. To some extent a portfolio formalises their own note-taking and record-keeping as they progress through the course. There have been student concerns about the diversity of portfolios, both in terms of the apparently different expectations of different tutors, and in terms of widely differing formats and amount of effort put into portfolio preparation on the part of students. More detailed guidelines were issued to students when these concerns arose, and as students progress through the course they begin to accept the diversity and concentrate more on what they wish to gain from their portfolio, rather than making comparisons with other students.

There have been problems in getting sufficient time for students and tutors to meet on a one-to-one basis both prior to and after portfolio completion. On a part-time course it is difficult to set up such meetings and hence sometimes students have submitted portfolios without prior negotiation of criteria for assessment. On occasions students have received only written tutor feedback on their portfolios with no opportunity for discussion.

Where students have failed to submit portfolios this has usually been because there were no firm deadlines. It has been left to option tutors to fix deadlines and some have taken the view that students should themselves determine when they are ready to synthesize their learning and submit it for tutor comment and that a single deadline for all students would be artificial and unproductive. However, most course team members are now coming to the view that busy part-time students in the main prefer to work to deadlines. Without clear deadlines, record-keeping of students' progress through the course is also difficult.

Discussion

Under the current system a considerable amount of time is required for tutors to discuss with individual students their intentions regarding their portfolios and the criteria by which they wish them to be judged, and to provide formative feedback through discussion after the portfolio has been completed and assessed. Alternatives may have to be found, perhaps involving peer support and feedback, to reduce the need for one-to-one contact between tutors and students. There have also been concerns about the diversity of portfolios, and student concerns may well have been less easily assuaged if the portfolios had been part of the formal assessment for the course rather than for formative feedback purposes. More detailed guidelines could be produced, but this might prove too restrictive since the high degree of student choice and independence seems to contribute greatly to the success of the portfolio approach on this course.

Students are very much in control of the activities they undertake to complete portfolios and generally find it a personally relevant process. This, together with the requirement to use portfolio material in the final assessed composite assignment, has been sufficient to sustain students' commitment to portfolios. The portfolio approach has succeeded in engaging students in reflection on their own learning which is an important course objective.

Note. The course is described here in the form it took before the University of Northumbria introduced a unitized scheme in 1994.

Bibliography

Bawden, R. J. and C. McKinnon, (1980), 'The Portfolio', Higher Education Research and Development Society of Australasia

Brown, S. and P. Maher, (1992), *Using Portfolios for Assessment: a guide for enterprising students*, Red Guides: Series 2, Newcastle: Northumbria University

Forrest, A. (1990), *Time Will Tell: Portfolio Assisted Assessment of General Education*, Washington: American Association for Higher Education

O'Brien, K. (1990), *Portfolio Assessment at Alverno College*, Milwaukee: Alverno College Institute

Payne, R. N., I. M. Robinson, C. Short, D. E. Eaton and D. H. Tidmarsh, (1992), 'A portfolio assessment scheme in engineering courses', in *Innovative Assessment in Higher Education*, University of Wales at Bangor

Tallantyre, F. (1992), *Portfolios as assessment tools within higher education*, Red Guides: Series 2,1, Newcastle: Northumbria University